A Williamson **Little Hands** Book

All Around Town

Exploring Your Community Through Craft Fun

by Judy Press

Illustrations
by Karen Weiss

WILLIAMSON PUBLISHING CHARLOTTE, VERMONT

Library of Congress Cataloging-in-Publication Data

Press, Judy, 1944–
   All around town : exploring your community through craft fun / Judy Press. ;
illustrations by Karen Weiss.
      p. cm. -- (A Williamson Little Hands book)
   Includes index.
   Summary: Explores the library, police station, park, post office, and other parts of a neighborhood through craft activities such as making a butterfly book bag, paper airplane, puppy puppet, and more.
   ISBN: 1-885593-68-6 (pbk.)
   1. Community--Juvenile literature. 2. Neighborhood--Juvenile literature. 3. Handicraft--Juvenile literature. 4. Creative activities and seat work--Juvenile literature. [1. Neighborhood. 2. Handicraft.] I. Title. II. Series.

HM756 .P74 2002
307--dc21

                                                2002023456

Little Hands® series editor: **Susan Williamson**
Interior and cover design: **Marie Ferrante–Doyle**
Interior Illustrations: **Karen Weiss**
Cover photo: **Peter J. Coleman**
Printing: **Capital City Press**

Williamson Publishing Co.
P.O. Box 185 • Charlotte, VT 05445
(800) 234-8791

Manufactured in the United States of America

10 9 8 7 6 5 4 3 2 1

Kids Can!®, *Little Hands*®, *Kaleidoscope Kids*®, and *Tales Alive!*® are registered trademarks of Williamson Publishing.

Good Times™, *Quick Starts for Kids!*™, and *You Can Do It!*™ are trademarks of Williamson Publishing.

Dedication

To my Aunt Annie, with love
from her favorite niece.

Acknowledgments

I wish to thank the following people for their support and encouragement in the writing of this book: the Mt. Lebanon Public Library and its children's librarians; the South Hills writers group; my talented friends, Carol Baicker-Mckee and Andrea Perry; my husband, Allan; my children, Brian Joseph and Aliza, Debbie and Mark, Darren and Lara, and Matt; and my cherished granddaughter, Anaelle.

This book would not have been possible without the talent and dedication of the following people at Williamson Publishing: Susan and Jack Williamson, Dana Pierson, Emily Stetson, Vicky Congdon, Jean Silveira, Julie Farrington, and Merietta McKenzie. A special thanks to designer Marie Ferrante-Doyle and illustrator Karen Weiss for their creative talents.

Permissions

Permission to use art from the following Williamson Publishing authors and illustrators is granted: Betsy Day, Laura Check, Michael Kline, Norma Jean Martin-Jourdensais, and Lynn M. Rosenblatt.

Contents

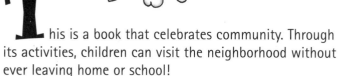

A Message to Grown-Ups

This is a book that celebrates community. Through its activities, children can visit the neighborhood without ever leaving home or school!

Children will become familiar with the roles of people and places in their towns or cities. They will learn how community workers keep us safe, discover what goes on inside the buildings, and explore ways to become better citizens.

The sections in this book entitled **"When I grow up"** describe the professions of the many people children encounter in their daily lives. **"Be a good neighbor"** encourages children to create links with others through helping behaviors, offering ways to help others and benefit the greater community by volunteering, recycling, and sharing ideas and creativity.

Materials & Crafts

The materials needed to complete the projects are readily available, and the directions are easy to follow. Crafts are meant to be embellished in each child's unique way. Avoid holding up perfectly completed projects as these tend to intimidate the young crafter and stifle creativity. Encourage new ideas, fanciful designs, and individualized interpretations so that each piece of art reflects the sensitivity and mood of the child who made it.

Some projects are more challenging than others. The house symbol next to each project will guide you: One house is the least challenging, and three houses may require more time and help.

Always remember to work in a well-ventilated room, assess your young crafter's propensity to put small objects into his mouth (choose materials accordingly), and work with nontoxic materials. Remember that younger siblings may pick up odds and ends from the floor or pull items off the table's edge. When scissors are used, please use child safety scissors, never sharp adult scissors.

Read the instruction aloud, just as you would read a storybook. Let the children ask and answer questions, and talk as they make the craft. Show children that reading directions is part of why we like to read! Through art, crafts, and exploration, we can share the joy of learning together.

Welcome to Our Town

Where do you live? In a small town or a big city? Do you walk to school or take the bus? Wherever you live, your home is part of a neighborhood. The people who live and work there are your neighbors.

In this book, you'll discover the many places in your community, the people who work there, and the tools they use. You'll imagine what you want to be when you grow up, and you'll dress up and make-believe. You'll learn ways to be a good neighbor and ways to stay safe. And when you're done crafting and playing, you can lay out all the things you've made for a play town. You can even add your own toy cars, trucks, and people. I know you'll have lots of fun, all around town!

MY HOME

"**T**here's no place like home." Have you ever heard someone say that?

All over the world, there are different kinds of homes — some people live in houses, some in apartments.

Others live in tents, tepees, or huts made out of grass or mud. But no matter what kind of dwelling you live in, it can be a wonderful place — a place that you know very well!

Peek-a-Boo House

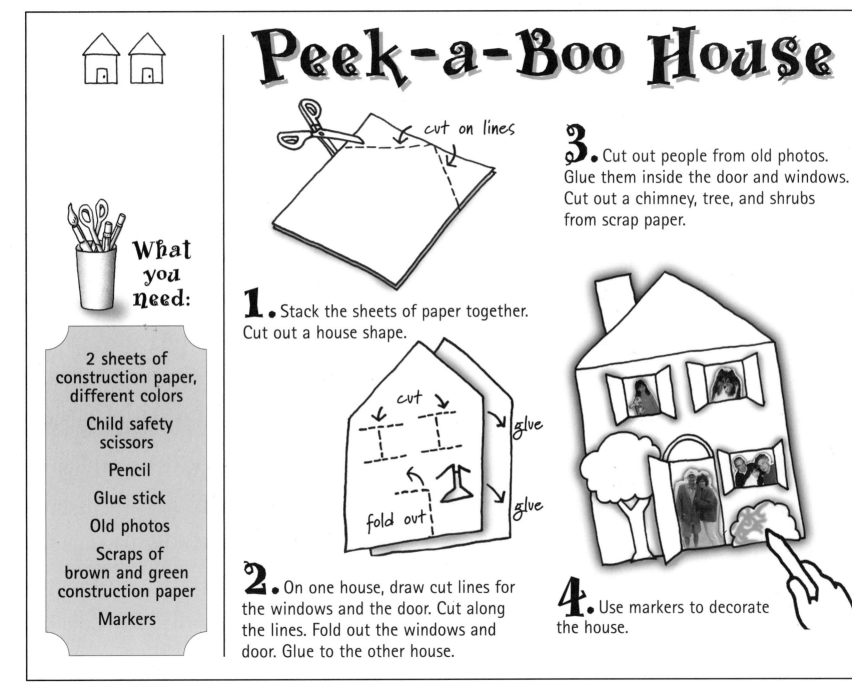

What you need:

2 sheets of construction paper, different colors

Child safety scissors

Pencil

Glue stick

Old photos

Scraps of brown and green construction paper

Markers

cut on lines

1. Stack the sheets of paper together. Cut out a house shape.

cut

fold out

glue

glue

2. On one house, draw cut lines for the windows and the door. Cut along the lines. Fold out the windows and door. Glue to the other house.

3. Cut out people from old photos. Glue them inside the door and windows. Cut out a chimney, tree, and shrubs from scrap paper.

4. Use markers to decorate the house.

Be a good neighbor!

Go on a neighborhood litter patrol with a grown-up. Wear gloves and take along a trash bag to pick up litter. Don't forget to recycle what you find.

When I grow up ...

I'll be an architect. Architects plan and design buildings.

- **Draw a picture of a pretend house.** Does it have lots of windows? A porch? Several floors or just one level? Where would your room be?

- **Build a tower from wooden building blocks** (no glue). Count how many blocks you can stack before it tumbles down!

Little Hands Story Corner™

Read *A Castle on Viola Street* by DyAnne DiSalvo to find out how an abandoned house can be turned into a home.

My Very Own Street Map

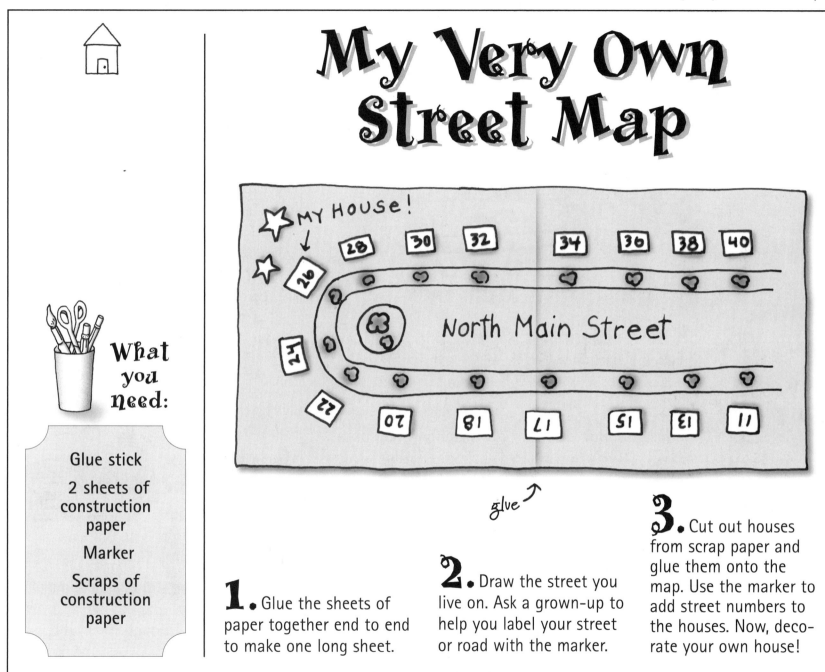

glue ↗

What you need:

Glue stick

2 sheets of construction paper

Marker

Scraps of construction paper

1. Glue the sheets of paper together end to end to make one long sheet.

2. Draw the street you live on. Ask a grown-up to help you label your street or road with the marker.

3. Cut out houses from scrap paper and glue them onto the map. Use the marker to add street numbers to the houses. Now, decorate your own house!

Be a good neighbor!

With your neighbors' permission, **write down phone numbers** and **names of people** who live in the houses on your street or in your apartment building. Ask a grown-up to make copies of your map and hand it out to your neighbors so they can get to know each other.

When I grow up ... **I'll be a mapmaker.** Someone who makes maps is called a *cartographer*. There are many different types of maps. A *street map* is a plan of the streets and buildings in a town or city.

- **Look for your city, town, or neighborhood on a map.** Find the nearest park, lake, or mountain. What roads do you travel to get to school?

- **Draw a map of your bedroom.** Don't forget to draw your bed, closet, and window.

- **Make a cardboard play mat.** Ask a grown-up to cut a large piece of cardboard from a carton. Draw the map of a town with tempera paint. Paint roads, buildings, and other places. Allow to dry. Travel around the city with your toy cars and trucks.

Little Hands Story Corner™

Read *It's My City: A Singing Map* to learn about the sights and sounds that a little girl and boy see and hear as they travel through their city.

SCHOOL

If you are in school, you're probably enjoying new games, making new friends, meeting new teachers, and learning many new things!

Think about all the exciting things that you do at school every day.

What is your favorite?

My New School

What you need:

Child safety scissors

Brown paper grocery bag

Empty cereal box

Tape

Construction paper

Glue

Markers

1. Cut open the paper bag and cut off the bottom. Lay the bag flat.

2. Wrap the box inside. Tape to hold.

3. Cut windows, doors, steps, and shrubs from construction paper. Glue them onto the front of the box.

4. Use markers to decorate the school.

Be a good neighbor!

Invite a grown-up to come visit your school (you'll have to ask your parents and teacher if it's OK first). Then, show that special person where everything is and some of the creative things you've made at school!

When I grow up ...

I'll be a schoolteacher. Schoolteachers help kids learn how to read and spell, do math, and find out cool stuff about the world we all live in!

• **Make a blackboard.** Glue black construction paper onto stiff cardboard for a classroom chalkboard. Use chalk to write on the board. What letters and numbers do you already know?

• **Pack a school lunch.** Use crayons and markers to draw designs on a paper lunch bag. Glue on stickers. Make sure you have your name on it, too. Then, join your friends for a picnic, indoors or out!

Little Hands Story Corner™

Read *Annabelle Swift, Kindergartner* by Amy Schwartz to learn how the lessons from an older sister help make Annabelle's first day in kindergarten a success.

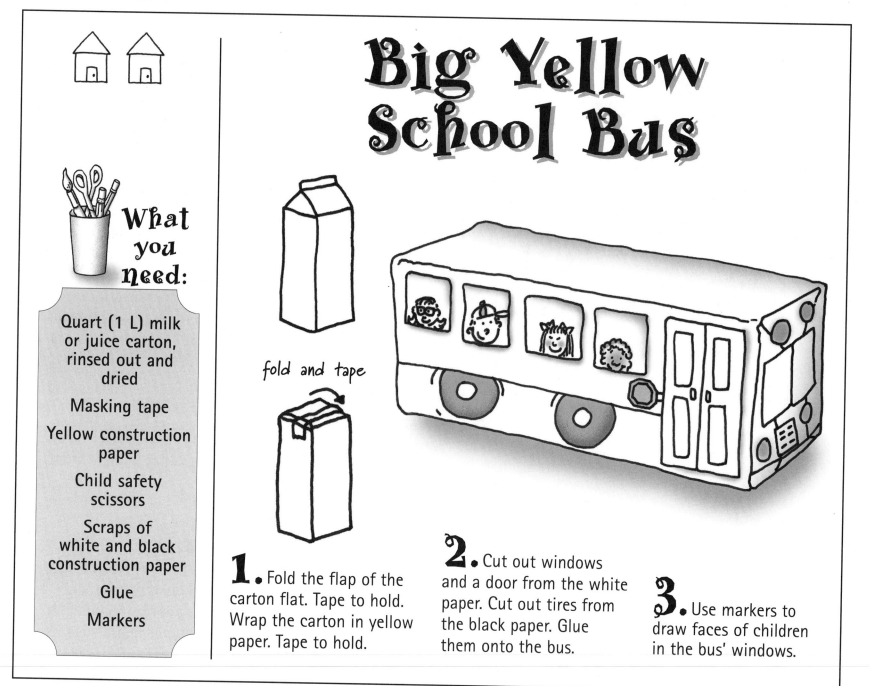

Big Yellow School Bus

What you need:

Quart (1 L) milk or juice carton, rinsed out and dried

Masking tape

Yellow construction paper

Child safety scissors

Scraps of white and black construction paper

Glue

Markers

fold and tape

1. Fold the flap of the carton flat. Tape to hold. Wrap the carton in yellow paper. Tape to hold.

2. Cut out windows and a door from the white paper. Cut out tires from the black paper. Glue them onto the bus.

3. Use markers to draw faces of children in the bus' windows.

Be a good neighbor!

Talk to grown-ups and younger siblings about school-bus safety rules. Then, practice the rules. Some of these you may know already. Great!

- Sit in your seat.
- Wait in line to get on and off the bus. No pushing, please!
- Always wait for the driver to tell you when it's safe to get off the school bus.
- Look up at the driver before crossing in front of the bus. Then, look both ways before crossing a street.
- Never bend down near or under the bus — the driver can't see you!

Thank you for being safe!

When I grow up ...

I'll be a school-bus driver. School-bus drivers transport children to and from school. The driver uses the lights, turn signals, horn, brakes, and rearview mirrors to make sure that the ride is a safe one.

- **Pretend play.** Line chairs up for a pretend bus ride. Sing and act out "The Wheels on the Bus" (page 16).

- **Make a double-decker bus,** using two milk cartons. Glue one carton on top of the other.

Little Hands Story Corner™

Read *School Bus* by Donald Crews.

The Wheels on the Bus

Try this fun action song while playing with your big yellow school bus.

To the tune of "The Wheels on the Bus," repeating motions throughout the verses.

1. The wheels on the bus go round and round,
   (turn hands in a circle)

   Round and round, round and round,

   The wheels on the bus go round and round,

   All through the town.

2. The kids on the bus go up and down —
   (stand up tall and then crouch down)

3. The doors on the bus go open and shut —
   (hands apart and together)

4. The driver on the bus says, "Move on back!" —
   (thumb over shoulder motion)

5. The wipers on the bus go *swish, swish, swish* —
   (move forearms back and forth like windshield wipers)

6. The horn on the bus goes *beep, beep, beep* —
   (pull or press "horn")

7. The brakes on the bus go *eek, eek, eek* —
   (push foot down as if stepping on brake)

8. The children on the bus go *yak, yak, yak* —
   (fingers to thumb in talking motion)

What other verses can you think of?

POLICE STATION

Our "men and women in blue" — that's what police officers are called — help out in so many ways that it's hard to count them all!

They keep our communities safe and are always on the scene when there's any trouble. They help when there's been an accident, and they help us to find our way when we're lost.

What other ways do police in your neighborhood help out?

Bright, Shiny Badge

What you need:

Pencil

Small white paper plate

Child safety scissors

Recycled aluminum foil

Scrap of black construction paper

Glue

Masking tape

Safety pin

1. Draw a badge on the paper plate. Cut it out.

2. Cover the badge with foil.

paper-plate piece

paper

foil

3. Cut out a number from the black construction paper. Glue it onto the badge.

4. Tape the pin to the back of the badge, so you can proudly wear it.

BACK

tape

When I grow up ...

I'll be a police officer. Police officers help protect the lives and property of people in a community by making sure everyone obeys the *laws* (rules). Police officers help out when there is a problem or emergency, such as a traffic accident. They also patrol neighborhoods to prevent crime, investigate complaints, and arrest or ticket those who "break the law" and don't follow the rules.

Be a good neighbor!

Do you know what to do in an emergency? You call a special number: **9-1-1**. Talk to grown-ups about when to use **9-1-1** and then ask them to help you make practice calls using a play telephone.

Little Hands Story Corner™

Read *Officer Buckle and Gloria* by Peggy Rathmann. In what ways do animals help people?

Police Officer's Ticket Book

1. Cut out a 4" x 7" (10 x 17.5 cm) rectangle from the cardboard. Cut sheets of white paper the same size.

7" (17.5 cm)

4" (10 cm)

Ticket Book

What you need:

Child safety scissors

Ruler

Cereal-box cardboard

White paper

Stapler

Black marker

2. Fold the cardboard in half. Fold the white paper in half. Ask a grown-up to help staple the white paper inside the cardboard for a ticket book.

3. Use the marker to decorate the book. Now, write a ticket!

Be a good neighbor!

Ask your teacher to invite a **police officer** to come to your pre-school or school. Ask the officer a lot of questions about her job.

Fingerprint fun. Fingerprints are one way police officers can keep track of different people. They can help prove that a person committed a crime, and they can also help find someone who is lost. Just for fun, take your own fingerprints!

Cut a sponge to fit inside a plastic margarine tub. Wet the sponge with paint for a printing pad. Press your fingertip into the pad; then, press your painted finger onto the paper. Compare your fingerprints to those of a friend. Are they the *same* or *different?*

Little Hands Story Corner™

Read *Policeman Small* by Lois Lenski. The book describes the daily duties of a corner traffic cop.

I'm a Police officer

Have fun with this action song while you wear your badge (page 18)!

To the tune of "I'm a Little Teapot."

I'm a police officer, with my star,

I help people near and far,
(point near you, then far away)

If you have a problem, call on me,
(point to self with thumb)

I'm your friend, as you can see.
(point to another child)

LIBRARY

Did you know that you can go anywhere in the world, anytime you want to? All you need is a book and your imagination. That's why the library is such an exciting place!

You can read about places to go, the people who live there, the music they play, the pets they have, or the animals that live near them. Imagine — the whole world in one building.

That's why the library is my favorite place in town!

My Local Library

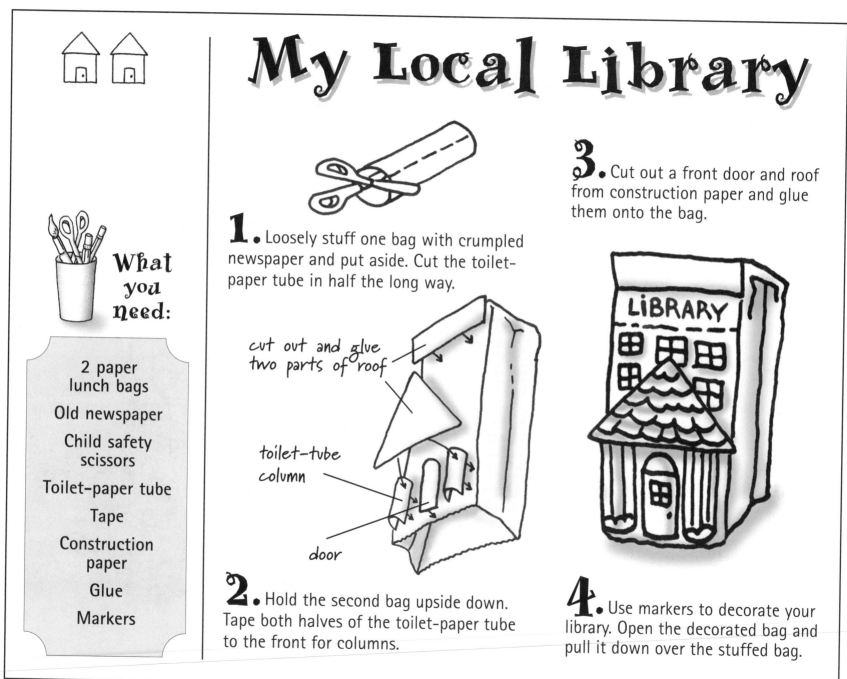

What you need:

2 paper lunch bags

Old newspaper

Child safety scissors

Toilet-paper tube

Tape

Construction paper

Glue

Markers

1. Loosely stuff one bag with crumpled newspaper and put aside. Cut the toilet-paper tube in half the long way.

cut out and glue two parts of roof

toilet-tube column

door

2. Hold the second bag upside down. Tape both halves of the toilet-paper tube to the front for columns.

3. Cut out a front door and roof from construction paper and glue them onto the bag.

LIBRARY

4. Use markers to decorate your library. Open the decorated bag and pull it down over the stuffed bag.

Be a good neighbor!

Ask friends and family to come to a **Book-Swap Party.** Have each person bring a used book to give away. Trade books, so that each person takes a different book home. Give your guests a home-made bookmark (see left) as they leave!

When I grow up ...

I'll be a librarian. Librarians select and order books, magazines, newspapers, CDs, and videos for the library so that people in town can borrow them. Then they put the books and other items back in the right places on the shelves when they are returned. Librarians answer lots of questions and help readers find what they need.

• **Make a bookmark.** Glue pictures from recycled greeting cards onto construction-paper strips for bookmarks.

Little Hands Story Corner™

Read *Book! Book! Book!* by Deborah Bruss. When the children go back to school, the farm animals are bored, so they go to the library to find something to read!

Butterfly Book Bag

What you need:

- Plain canvas tote bag
- Old newspaper
- Sharp scissors (for grown-up use only)
- Sponge
- Fabric paint
- Paper plate
- Fabric paint in easy-squeeze bottles

1. Lay the canvas bag on a flat surface. Put a few sheets of newspaper inside. Ask a grown-up to help you cut a butterfly shape or other shape from the sponge.

2. Pour a thin layer of fabric paint into the plate. Dip the sponge into the paint. Press the sponge shape onto the bag to make prints.

3. Use fabric paints in squeeze bottles to outline and decorate the pressed shapes. Let the bag dry completely before using.

When I grow up ... I'll be an author.

Authors express their ideas, thoughts, and feelings by writing stories, poems, and essays.

• **Make up a story** about an imaginary character. A pretend story is called *fiction*. Now, tell a story about something that really happened. That story is called *nonfiction*. Ask a grown-up to write down your stories or record them on a tape player.

• **Make a bookcase.** Gather three large cardboard boxes. Boxes about 9" x 10" x 13" (22.5 x 25 x 32.5 cm) work well. Stack the boxes or place them side by side for bookshelves. Sort your books by *kind* (animal stories, science stories, fairy stores, and so on), by *author* (the name of the person who wrote it, like Dr. Seuss), or by *series* (the Berenstain Bears books, for instance). Stack the books neatly in your bookcase.

Be a good neighbor!

Get your own library card! Then, visit your library often. Ask the librarian to help you pick out books to read. (Don't forget to return them on time!) Attend a story hour or other program at your library, too.

Little Hands Story Corner™

Read *Tomas and the Library Lady* by Pat Mora to find out how a boy who picks fruits and vegetables with his family far from their home visits the local public library and learns everything he can about the world.

FIRE STATION

Firefighters sure are brave! These men and women save lives and property (and pets!) every day. They rescue people when there's a fire, and they visit homes and schools to teach fire safety.

Ask a grown-up to take you to visit your local fire station. You might even get to sit in a fire truck!

Friendly Fire Station

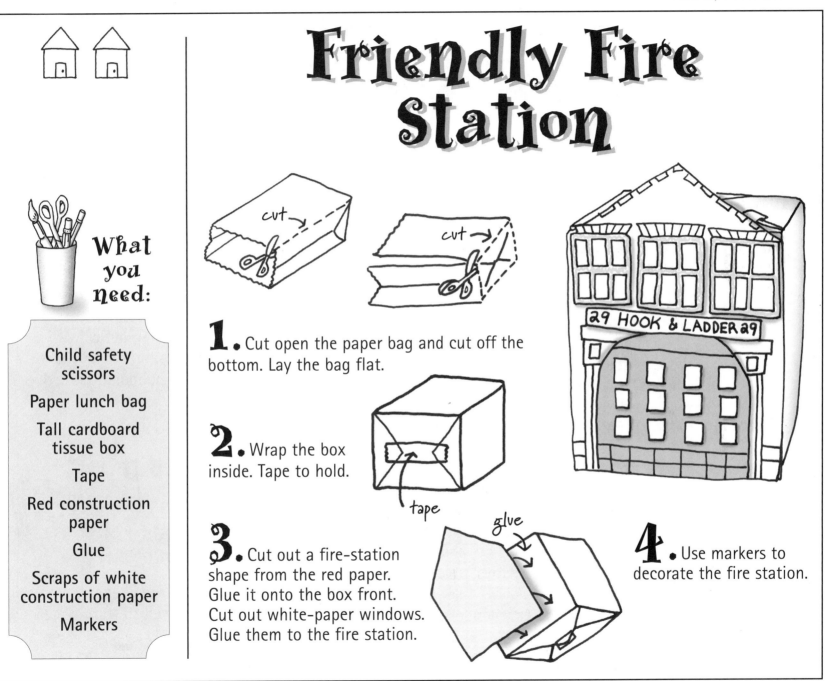

What you need:

Child safety scissors

Paper lunch bag

Tall cardboard tissue box

Tape

Red construction paper

Glue

Scraps of white construction paper

Markers

1. Cut open the paper bag and cut off the bottom. Lay the bag flat.

2. Wrap the box inside. Tape to hold.

3. Cut out a fire-station shape from the red paper. Glue it onto the box front. Cut out white-paper windows. Glue them to the fire station.

4. Use markers to decorate the fire station.

cut

cut

tape

glue

29 HOOK & LADDER 29

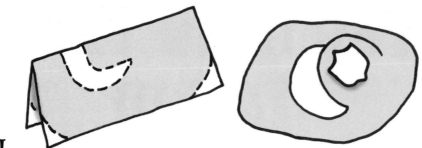

When I grow up ...

I'll be a firefighter. Firefighters put out fires and save people from burning buildings. A firefighter's hat is slanted down the back. Can you guess why? It's so water can drain off the firefighter's head!

• **Make your own firefighter's hat.** Fold a sheet of construction paper in half the long way. Cut away the corners opposite the fold and then cut part of a circle into the folded edge (don't cut the whole circle out, though). Lay the paper flat and bend the center flap up. Cut a badge from foil and glue it onto the flap. Try your hat on. Make the center hole bigger if needed.

Pass the Buckets

Before there were fire engines, people used large leather buckets filled with water to fight fires. When a fire broke out, townspeople would run with their buckets and form two towlines between the fire and the nearest source of water. Buckets of water would be passed up one line; then, the water was thrown on the fire, and the empty buckets were passed down the other line to be refilled.

Be a good neighbor!

Where are the smoke alarms in your house? Ask a grown-up to check all of the household smoke alarms and replace the batteries if necessary. Now, talk about what you should do in case there's ever a real fire. Then, practice with a pretend fire drill! Remind your friends and neighbors to practice fire drills, too.

Little Hands Story Corner™

Read *Clifford the Firehouse Dog* by Norman Bridwell to learn more about fire safety.

Big Red Fire Engine

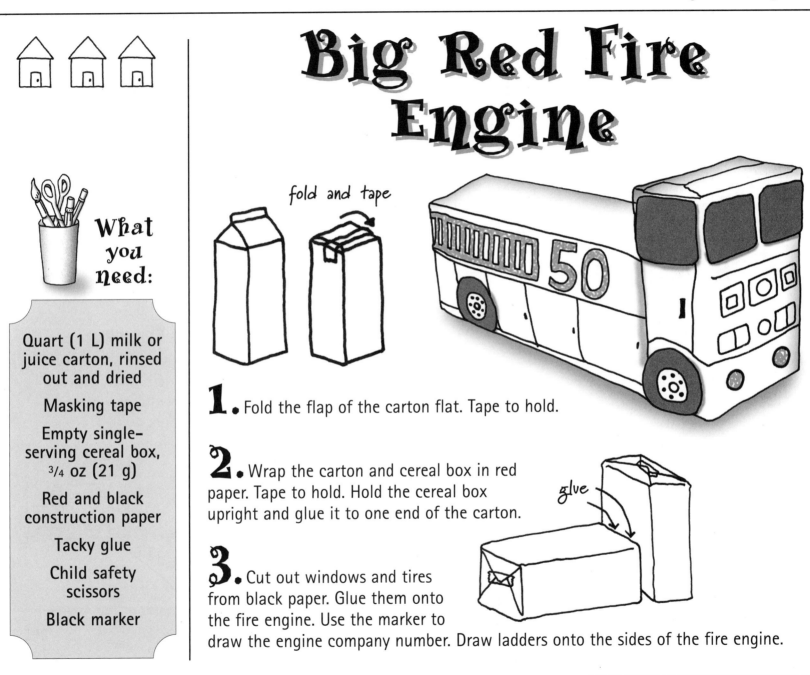

fold and tape

What you need:

Quart (1 L) milk or juice carton, rinsed out and dried

Masking tape

Empty single-serving cereal box, ³/₄ oz (21 g)

Red and black construction paper

Tacky glue

Child safety scissors

Black marker

1. Fold the flap of the carton flat. Tape to hold.

2. Wrap the carton and cereal box in red paper. Tape to hold. Hold the cereal box upright and glue it to one end of the carton.

glue

3. Cut out windows and tires from black paper. Glue them onto the fire engine. Use the marker to draw the engine company number. Draw ladders onto the sides of the fire engine.

Be a good neighbor!

Teach your friends and family how to stop, drop, and roll. If your clothes catch on fire:

STOP: Stop where you are. Don't run.

DROP: Drop to the ground.

ROLL: Roll back and forth to smother the flames, protecting your face with your hands.

When I grow up ...

I'll be a fire marshal. Fire marshals take care of fire prevention. They inspect buildings to make sure they are safe. They talk to schoolchildren about fire safety and how to keep a fire from getting started.

• **Teamwork** is an important part of learning to be a firefighter. Everyone must work together as part of a team. Practice teamwork at your next family dinner. Have one person plan the meal and cook it. Another person can set the table. When the meal is over, assign someone to clear the table and another person to do the dishes. Wow! Teamwork really helps get things done!

Little Hands Story Corner™

Read *The Little Fire Engine* by Lois Lenski to learn what happens when firefighter Small rushes to put out a fire in his town.

The Brave Firefighters

Try this firefighter fingerplay as you pretend to answer a fire alarm!
Don't forget your fire hat (page 30)!

Five brave firefighters sit so still,
(hold up four fingers and thumb)
Until they spot a fire on top of the hill,
(shade eyes with hand and look around)
Number one rings the bell, ding-dong!
(hands clasped high and then low, like a ringing bell)
Number two pulls some black boots on,
(pull hands up legs)
Number three jumps on the fire engine red,
(jump in place)
Number four puts a fire hat on her head,
(hands on head)
Number five drives the red fire truck,
(pretend to drive)
Turn left and right so you don't get stuck!
(sway left and right)
Whoooo! Whooo! Hear the fire truck say,
As all of the cars get out of its way,
(move arms as if pushing something aside)

Whish! Goes the water from the fire hose spout,
(rub palms together)
And quicker than a wink, the fire is out!
(clap hands)

PARK

It doesn't matter what time of year it is, the park is always a wonderful place!

Does the park in your town have trees and flowers? Some parks have a swing set or climbing structure. A bike path or walking trail with benches to sit on is nice, too. Ball playing fields or basketball courts sure are fun!

What do you like to do at the park?

Rocking Seesaw

loop for head

twist for body

bend for hands and feet

What you need:

3 pipe cleaners

Child safety scissors

Small white paper plate

Markers

Tape

1. Bend the first pipe cleaner in half so a loop forms in the top (head). Twist the cleaner below the loop to make the body. Bend the ends for feet. Repeat with the second pipe cleaner to make a second body.

2. Cut the third pipe cleaner in half. To make the arms, wrap a piece below the "head" loop on each pipe-cleaner body. Bend the ends for hands.

3. Decorate the paper plate with markers. Fold it in half for a seesaw. Tape your pipe-cleaner friends to each side of the seesaw.

When I grow up ...

I'll be a camp counselor. Counselors take kids at day camps, park programs, and overnight camps on hikes and nature walks. They also teach kids to swim, ride horses, play tennis, paddle or sail a boat, do gymnastics, and dance. And, they also know a lot of games. Try these two:

• **Seesaw.** You'll need two players for this game. Players sit facing one another, with legs spread apart, overlapping their partner's. Partners hold hands and seesaw back and forth.

• **Leap frog.** Crouch down and, with your hands on your ankles, try leaping like a frog as you say this rhyme.

"Leap frog, leap frog,

Easy as can be;

I'll leap with you,

And you leap with me.

Leap frog, leap frog,

On your lily pad;

You can leap farther,

And you're so glad!"

Be a good neighbor!

With a grown-up's permission and help, **invite some neighborhood kids over for a day of mini-camp** in your backyard. Have fun playing games, singing songs, and doing art and crafts. You can even make up your own camp song!

Little Hands Story Corner™

Read *Pippi Longstocking in the Park* by Astrid Lingren for some playful park adventures!

Popsicle Trees

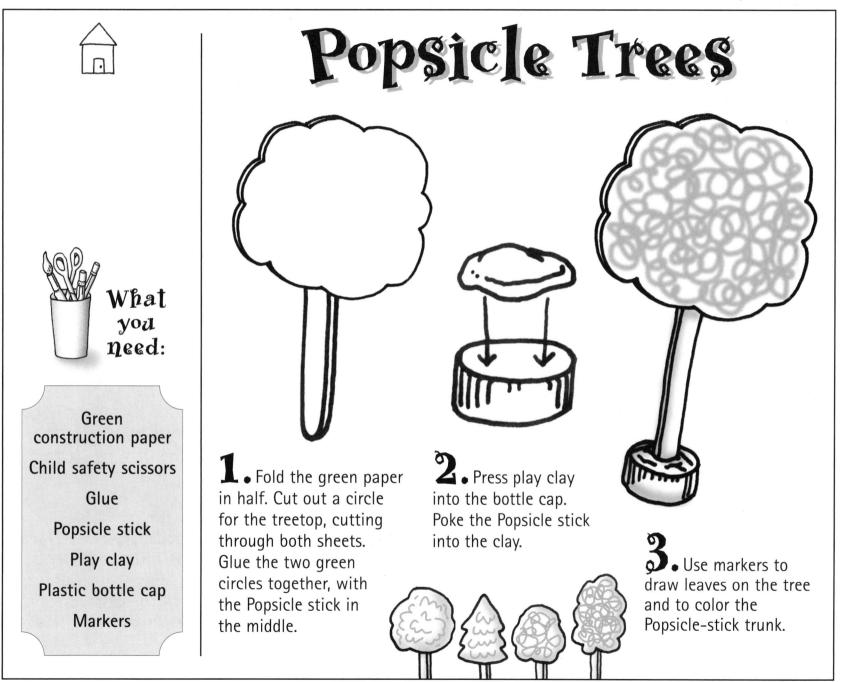

What you need:

Green construction paper

Child safety scissors

Glue

Popsicle stick

Play clay

Plastic bottle cap

Markers

1. Fold the green paper in half. Cut out a circle for the treetop, cutting through both sheets. Glue the two green circles together, with the Popsicle stick in the middle.

2. Press play clay into the bottle cap. Poke the Popsicle stick into the clay.

3. Use markers to draw leaves on the tree and to color the Popsicle-stick trunk.

Be a good neighbor!

Go to <**www.kidsdomain.com/holiday/earthday**> to learn ways to be good to the earth. One way is to ask friends and family to help you collect trash in and around your park so it can be green and clean!

When I grow up ...

I'll be a landscape architect. Landscape architects design places such as public parks and playgrounds. They arrange flowers, shrubs, trees, benches, walkways, and structures so that these areas are beautiful to look at and work well together. Landscape architects also help people design areas for playing, sitting, and gardening in their own yards.

• **Place leaves** from different trees under thin sheets of paper; then, rub a crayon over the tops for leaf rubbings. Staple sheets together for a book about trees.

•**Look closely** at the trees that grow in your neighborhood. What is the shape of the leaves? Is the bark smooth or rough? Compare the trees. Which ones are the *same* and which are *different?*

Little Hands Story Corner™

Read *The Apple Pie Tree* by Zoe Hall to learn more about apple trees. The *Great Kapok Tree* by Lynne Cherry and *The Giving Tree* by Shel Silverstein are two good stories about what we can learn from trees.

I'm a Tall, Tall Tree

Here is a great fingerplay to help you enjoy the seasons
with your Popsicle trees (page 37)!

This is my trunk, *(point to body)*
I'm a tall, tall tree. *(hold arms up like branches)*
In the springtime, the blossoms *(make fists)*
Cover me.
They open, they open. *(open fingers)*

This is my trunk, *(point to body)*
I'm a tall, tall tree. *(hold arms up like branches)*
In the summer, the breezes
Blow through me.
   (raise arms and wave them back and forth)
I bend, I bend. *(sway back and forth)*

This is my trunk, *(point to body)*
I'm a tall, tall tree. *(hold arms up like branches)*
In the autumn, the apples
   (form circles with thumbs and index fingers)
Form on me.
They drop, they drop. *(clap hands)*

This is my trunk, *(point to body)*
I'm a tall, tall tree. *(hold arms up like branches)*
In the winter, the snowflakes *(flutter fingers down)*
Land on me.
Brrr! Brrr! *(hug self and shiver)*

HOSPITAL

Have you ever visited the hospital? That's where people go if there is something wrong with their bodies that they can't fix at home.

Sometimes a visit can be short (if you fall out of a tree, for instance. Ouch!). Other times, a person might need an operation and stay for two or three days.

No matter how long your stay is, you can be sure there will be lots of people taking good care of you!

Amazing X-Ray Picture

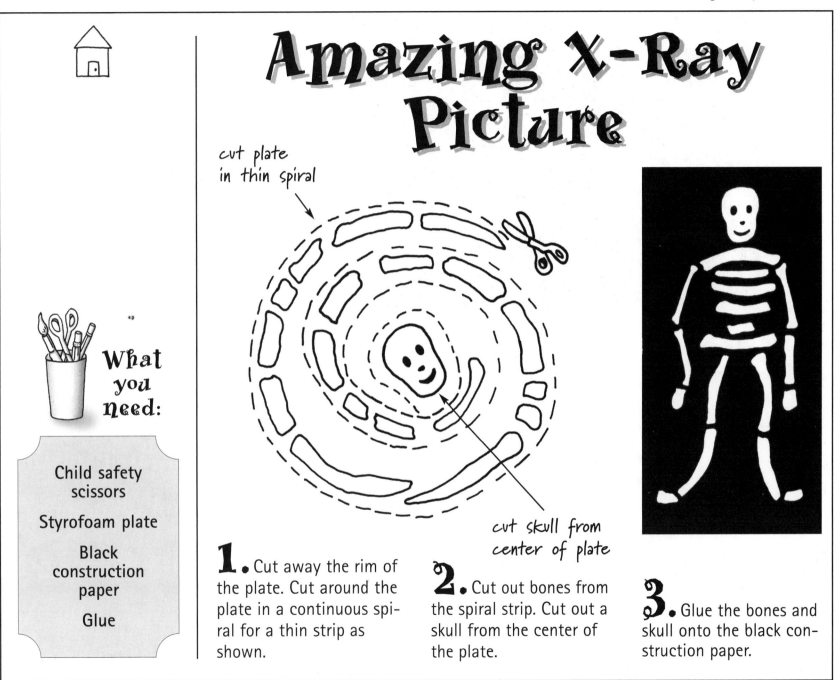

cut plate
in thin spiral

What you need:

Child safety scissors

Styrofoam plate

Black construction paper

Glue

cut skull from center of plate

1. Cut away the rim of the plate. Cut around the plate in a continuous spiral for a thin strip as shown.

2. Cut out bones from the spiral strip. Cut out a skull from the center of the plate.

3. Glue the bones and skull onto the black construction paper.

When I grow up ...

I'll be an x-ray technician. X-ray technicians take special pictures (*x-rays*) of parts of the inside of the human body. Doctors use x-rays to help them decide what medical problems patients may have.

• **Create an x-ray picture** of a dinosaur by gluing the strips of a Styrofoam plate onto black paper in the shape of a dinosaur. Then, do "x-rays" of other animals.

• **Make a first-aid kit.** Ask a grown-up to help you fill a shoe box with ace bandages, Band-Aids, cotton balls, sterile pads, surgical tape, resealable plastic bags (for ice packs), and alcohol pads. Store it in a handy closet or in the car.

Be a good neighbor!

Fill a small bag with crayons, paper, stickers, books, and playing cards. **Give your "Get Well" bag to a friend** who's been sick or missed school.

Little Hands Story Corner™

Read *Doctor White* by Jane Goodall and find out what happens when a small white dog goes to the hospital to visit sick children.

Take-Around-Town Doctor's Bag

cut away ↗

What you need:

Child safety scissors

Brown paper grocery bag

Tape

Black construction paper

Scrap of cereal-box cardboard

cut out two handles from cardboard ↘

1. Cut away the top three-fourths of the grocery bag. Tape black construction paper to each side of the bottom.

2. Cut out two handles from the scrap cardboard. Cover the handles in black paper and tape to the bag.

Be a good neighbor!

Create a homemade "Get Well" card. Fold a sheet of paper in half. Decorate the front of the card and write a cheery greeting inside. Send your card to a neighbor or friend who is sick.

When I grow up ...

I'll be a doctor. Doctors take care of people who are sick. They also know how to help healthy people stay healthy.

• **There are many different kinds of doctors.** A *pediatrician* takes care of infants and children. Gather your stuffed animals for pretend patients. Help them to get well with bandages and lots of hugs!

• **Listen to your heartbeat.** A *stethoscope* lets a doctor listen to your heart and lungs. Hold the bottom of a paper cup against your ear. Press it against a friend's chest to hear his heartbeat. Then trade, and let your friend listen to your heartbeat!

Little Hands Story Corner™

Read *Goldie Locks Has Chicken Pox* by Erin Dealey for an amusing story about what it's like to be sick in bed when your friends want to play.

Foil-Mirror Headband

Here's an old-fashioned doctor's instrument that you can add to your bag. Doctors used to use these to look at things up close. Now they have big lights and fancy magnifying glasses to help them.

What you need: Construction paper, child safety scissors, tape, cereal-box cardboard, recycled aluminum foil, stapler

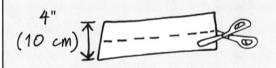

4"
(10 cm)

Cut out a paper band. Cut in half lengthwise.

Tape the short ends together. Fit the band around your head. Ask a grown-up to staple the ends to fit.

Cut out a round cardboard shape and wrap in foil.

Staple the round shape to the band.

ANIMAL SHELTER

Just like kids (and grown-ups!), animals need places where they can be safe, warm, and cared for. An animal shelter is where stray dogs and cats can be cared for until a family takes them home to love.

Many *volunteers* (people who give their time to help out) take care of the animals at the shelter, feeding, grooming, and taking the animals out for exercise. There are lots of pets there!

Playful Puppy Puppet

What you need:

Child safety scissors

Brown construction paper

Glue stick

Brown paper lunch bag

Wiggly eyes

Pom-pom

Brown marker

1. Cut out the puppy's ears, paws, and tail from the brown paper. Fold under the corners of the flap of the bag. Glue the ears onto the flap of the bag. Glue the paws onto the front of the bag. Glue the tail onto the back of the bag.

2. Glue on the puppy's wiggly eyes and pom-pom nose. Use the marker to draw the puppy's spots.

Be a good neighbor!

Volunteer, with a grown-up, at an **animal shelter** in your town. Ask if you can take a dog for a walk, hold a kitty, or feed the animals.

When I grow up ...

I'll be a veterinarian.

Veterinarians (also called "*vets*") are doctors who take care of animals. They treat cats, dogs, and other small animals in an examining room. If a cow or horse is sick, the vet will drive to visit it on the farm. Vets even visit animals at the zoo!

• **The vet uses a type of flashlight** to examine an animal to find out what is wrong. Use a flashlight to examine your stuffed animals. How do they look, doctor?

Little Hands Story Corner™

Read *Let's Get a Pup, Said Kate* by Bob Graham. What kind of animal would you choose to take home from an animal shelter?

Purr-fect Paw Prints

What you need:

Pencil

Small paper plate

Child safety scissors

Light-colored construction paper

Sponge

Black tempera paint, in a lid or dish

1. Draw a paw print in the center of the paper plate. Cut out the paw print without cutting into the rim of the plate. (Ask a grown-up to help you get started.)

2. Hold the paw-print stencil against the construction paper. Dip the sponge into the paint and dab it onto the stencil.

3. Lift the stencil and move it to another place on the paper. Repeat the paint dabbing. Let dry. Does it look as if a cat or dog walked across your paper?

When I grow up ...

I'll be a pet groomer. Pet groomers wash, comb, and trim the hair of dogs and cats. They also trim pets' nails.

• **Play a game of cat and mouse.** Players stand in a circle holding hands. Two players are chosen to be the cat and mouse. The cat chases the mouse around the outside of the circle. Whenever the mouse wants to enter or leave the circle, the players try to lower their arms so the cat can't follow. When the cat catches the mouse, other players take their turns to be cat and mouse.

• **Cut pictures of animals** from old magazines. Then, cut the pictures in half. Invent new animals by putting unmatched halves together.

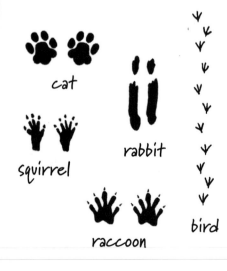

cat

squirrel

rabbit

raccoon

bird

• **Make "paw prints"** on steamy windows or mirrors. Press your palm and just the tips of your fingers.

• **Look for animal prints** after a snowfall or in the sand at the beach. Can you identify a bird's prints? How about cat or dog prints? Press your footprint in the snow or sand. How does it compare with an animal's print?

Be a good neighbor!

Ask a grown-up to help you **plan a neighborhood pet show.** Invite other kids and ask them to bring their pets. Set up categories for the biggest, smallest, cutest, best behaved, and best trick. Award the winners with homemade ribbons!

Little Hands Story Corner™

Read *My New Kitten* by Joanna Cole. If you had a new kitten, what would you name it?

Silly Kitty Mask

Wear your mask to prowl around,
exploring the sights and sounds in your home!

What you need:
Paper plate, sharp scissors
(for grown-up use only),
construction paper,
markers, glue,
pipe cleaners,
Popsicle or
craft stick

Cut construction-
paper ears.

Glue on
whiskers
and ears.

Cut
out
eye
holes.

Draw face;
color stripes.

Glue
mask
on
stick.

National Pet Week comes in early May. Most of us already take good care of our pets, but during this week we are especially kind and loving to our animal friends to let them know how much we appreciate them. What are some ways you could show your pet how special it is? If you don't have a pet, ask a neighbor or friend with a pet if you could bring it a special treat. You may get a big lick of thanks in return!

POST OFFICE

When you send someone a letter or get a birthday card in the mail, do you ever wonder how the mail gets from one place to the other? You can thank the workers at the post office!

In the United States, postal workers carry more mail to more people every day than they do in any other country in the world. Their motto is that nothing can stop them from delivering the mail — not even a big storm or a barking dog!

Colorful Sticker Stamps

1. Cut out a stamp shape from white paper. Use markers to decorate your stamp.

What you need:

Child safety scissors or decorative-edged scissors

White paper

Markers

Small paintbrush

Sticker Glue (see this page)

White envelope

2. Brush the Sticker Glue onto the back of the stamp. Let the glue dry. Use a drop of water to moisten the stamp. Then, stick it onto an envelope for pretend play.

Sticker Glue

¼ cup (50 ml) glue
1 tablespoon (15 ml) vinegar

Mix well. Brush onto paper.
Allow to dry.

When I grow up ...

I'll be a postal clerk. Postal clerks sort mail for delivery. They also sell stamps, weigh packages to figure out how much postage each one needs, and check that packages are wrapped carefully so they don't fall apart before they arrive.

• **Ask your friends and relatives** to save unusual stamps for you. Sort the stamps by the country they are from or by colors.

• **Cover a shoe box in recycled wrapping paper.** Ask a grown-up to cut a slit in the top and use it for a mailbox outside your room!

Be a good neighbor!

Recycle used greeting card fronts (make sure there's no message on the back). Donate them to:

St. Jude's Ranch for Children
100 St. Jude's Street
Boulder City, Nevada 89005-1618

The children at the ranch use the fronts to make new cards and then sell them to raise money for the ranch.

Little Hands Story Corner™

Read *Harvey Hare, Postman Extraordinaire* by Bernadette Watts, which tells the story of how the animals plan a perfect present for their postman.

Big Brown Mail Bag

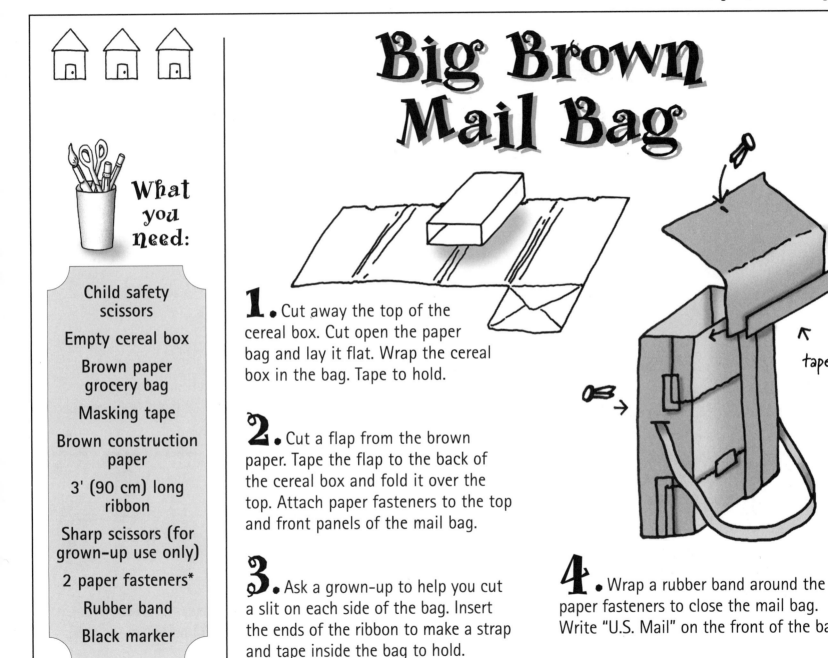

What you need:

Child safety scissors

Empty cereal box

Brown paper grocery bag

Masking tape

Brown construction paper

3' (90 cm) long ribbon

Sharp scissors (for grown-up use only)

2 paper fasteners*

Rubber band

Black marker

1. Cut away the top of the cereal box. Cut open the paper bag and lay it flat. Wrap the cereal box in the bag. Tape to hold.

2. Cut a flap from the brown paper. Tape the flap to the back of the cereal box and fold it over the top. Attach paper fasteners to the top and front panels of the mail bag.

3. Ask a grown-up to help you cut a slit on each side of the bag. Insert the ends of the ribbon to make a strap and tape inside the bag to hold.

tape

4. Wrap a rubber band around the paper fasteners to close the mail bag. Write "U.S. Mail" on the front of the bag.

*Caution: Paper fasteners pose a choking and poking danger to young children. Grown-ups should control the supply and insert them into the project.

Be a good neighbor!

With help from a grown-up, **offer your mail carrier a cold drink** on a hot day **or a hot drink** on a cold day. You could even tell him a joke (see below) to brighten his day!

. . . .

Tell a Postal Joke

A lady bought a stamp at the post office and asked the clerk, "Shall I stick it on myself?"

The clerk answered, "It'll get there faster if you stick it on the envelope." Yuk! Yuk!

. . . .

When I grow up ...

I'll be a mail carrier. Mail carriers deliver letters, packages, and magazines. They collect the mail from the post office, fill their bags, then go out and deliver it. Carriers in cities deliver the mail on foot. Carriers outside of town drive along their routes where houses are farther apart.

• **Fill your cereal-box mail bag** with letters you have written. Deliver your letters to friends and family.

• **Save piles of "junk mail."** Play a pretend game of post office and deliver the mail.

Little Hands Story Corner™

Read *Postal Workers* by Paulette Bourgeois and Kim LaFave to learn what happens when you mail a letter.

CONSTRUCTION SITE

Lots of people sure are working hard at the construction site! You can see all kinds of cool machines like 'dozers, cement mixers, cranes, and trucks moving dirt, rocks, and big steel beams around.

Inside the buildings, electricians put in wires so you can turn on lights and run your computer. The plumbers put in pipes for all the water that you need.

They're all working to build a wonderful new building for you to enjoy!

Toothpick Town

What you need:

Woden toothpicks

Glue

Black construction paper

1. Dip the ends of the toothpicks into glue.

2. Glue the toothpicks onto black construction paper in the shape of buildings. Break the toothpicks into smaller pieces if necessary.

When I grow up ...

I'll be a construction worker. Construction workers are part of the team that builds offices, highways, bridges, apartment buildings, and people's houses.

- **Build a miniature city** with different-sized cereal boxes and cardboard tubes. Paint them to represent buildings. A tall box could be a skyscraper and a smaller box could be your house.

- **Make a postcard puzzle.** On the back of an old postcard that shows a city or town, draw a zigzag line. Cut along the line for puzzle pieces.

- **Visit a construction site with a grown-up.** Construction workers work alongside carpenters, bricklayers, and stonemasons. What heavy equipment is on the site? Do you see a bulldozer, cement mixer, or a dump truck?

Hard Hats

No matter what kinds of jobs they do, all of the workers at construction sites wear big, yellow hard hats. Can you guess why construction workers' hats are so hard? That's right! If something falls from way up high — **bonk!** — no problem; the hats protect their heads.

Little Hands Story Corner™

Read *The Lot at the End of the Block* by Kevin Lewis. This is a story about the construction of a building from beginning to end. And if you don't know the story *Mike Mulligan and His Steam Shovel* by Virginia Lee Burton, you'll want to read that, too!

Tool Silhouettes

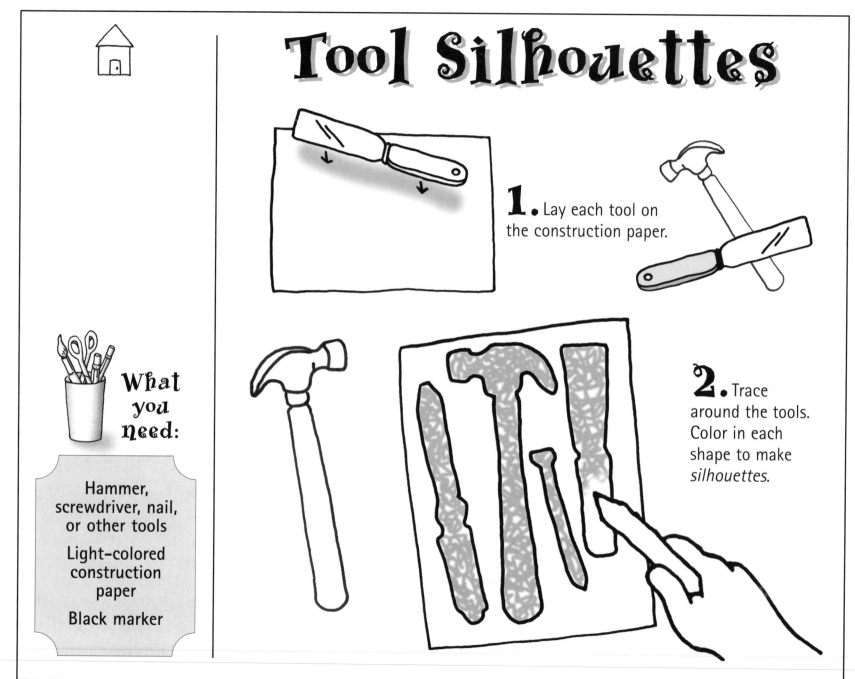

1. Lay each tool on the construction paper.

2. Trace around the tools. Color in each shape to make *silhouettes*.

What you need:

Hammer, screwdriver, nail, or other tools

Light-colored construction paper

Black marker

When I grow up ...

I'll be a carpenter. Carpenters build with wood and other materials, sawing, sanding, shaping pieces, and putting them all together. They work with *hand tools*, such as hammers, saws, screwdrivers, and tools that measure. They also work with *power tools*, like electric saws and drills.

• **Use a toy hammer or a block of wood** to hammer a golf tee into Styrofoam.

• **Use child safety scissors** to cut Styrofoam blocks into a variety of shapes and sizes. Build a Styrofoam sculpture using toothpicks to attach the blocks to each other.

• **See if your local library** has the video *Bob the Builder*. Watch it and imagine doing those tasks yourself!

Be a good neighbor!

If you borrow a tool from a grown-up or friend, be sure to return it promptly, and in good condition. The same goes for toys!

Sunny Silhouettes

On a nice day, lay a piece of dark construction paper in the sun. Lay your tools on the paper and come back in a few hours. Remove your tools from the paper. What do you see?

Little Hands Story Corner™

Read *Tools* by Claude Delafosse to discover how many tools work.

Construction fun!

Hammer away with this fun action song!

"Peter Hammers"

1. Peter works with one hammer, one hammer, one hammer,
   (pound one fist)

   Peter works with one hammer this fine day.

Repeat verses with added motions:

2. Peter works with two hammers —
   (pound two fists)

3. Peter works with three hammers —
   (pound two fists and one foot)

4. Peter works with four hammers —
   (pound two fists and two feet)

5. Peter works with five hammers —
   (pound two fists and two feet, and nod your head)

RAILROAD STATION

Fields, mountains, cities, and people in their neighborhoods — there's so much to see out the window of a train!

Some trains take very long trips across rivers and plains. You can sleep overnight on these trains and even put your car on the train so it arrives with you. Other trains travel only a short distance to take people to their jobs. Would you like to travel by train somewhere?

Clickety-Clack Train Track

What you need:

Glue

Popsicle sticks

Cardboard or heavy paper

Wooden toothpicks

1. Glue Popsicle sticks lengthwise on the cardboard.

2. Cover the Popsicle sticks with toothpicks placed crosswise.

3. Now make some trees (page 37) to put along your tracks. Play trains using your toys. Can you make the sound of the whistle?

Be a good neighbor!

On a crowded train, it's nice to **offer your seat** to a person who is physically challenged or elderly. Ask if you can sit in your mom or dad's lap or share your seat with a brother or sister. Now, there's more room for everyone to sit down!

When I grow up ... **I'll be a locomotive engineer.** Locomotive engineers operate large trains carrying cargo and passengers. Engineers receive starting instructions from conductors and move controls such as *throttles* and *air brakes* to drive their locomotives.

• **With your friends, go on a pretend train ride.** Line up a row of chairs. Take turns being the engineer who sits in the first chair and calls out, "All aboard!" Add sound effects: *choo-choo, chug-chug, whoo-whoo.* At each "stop," remove one chair (car), have the engineer move to the back of the train, and let the next person move up to the engineer's seat.

• **Sing the songs** "I've Been Working on the Railroad" and "Down by the Station," and act out the words!

Little Hands Story Corner™

Read the books *Freight Train* by Donald Crews, *Smokey* by Bill Peet, or *The Little Engine That Could* by Watty Piper.

"All Aboard!" Train

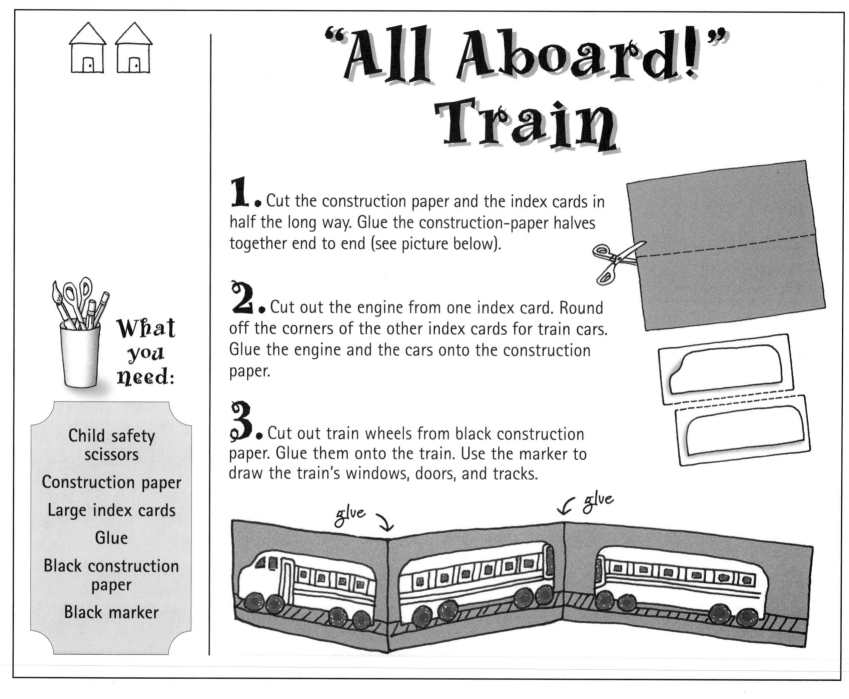

1. Cut the construction paper and the index cards in half the long way. Glue the construction-paper halves together end to end (see picture below).

2. Cut out the engine from one index card. Round off the corners of the other index cards for train cars. Glue the engine and the cars onto the construction paper.

3. Cut out train wheels from black construction paper. Glue them onto the train. Use the marker to draw the train's windows, doors, and tracks.

What you need:

Child safety scissors

Construction paper

Large index cards

Glue

Black construction paper

Black marker

glue ↓   ↙ glue

Be a good neighbor!

Tell your friends about railroad safety:

• Never play on or near a railroad track.

• When you are in a station, stand back from the tracks.

• Don't push or shove when getting on or off a train.

When I grow up ...

I'll be a railroad conductor. Railroad conductors make sure passengers on trains are safe and comfortable. They let the engineers (page 65) know when all of the passengers have *boarded* (gotten on). Then, they collect the tickets or *fares* (money) as the train leaves the station.

• **Make a tunnel from a paper grocery bag** (page 110). Place your tunnel over your toy train tracks (page 64). Watch your toy train go through the tunnel.

• **Cut out train tickets from construction paper.** Write a destination on the ticket. Use a hole punch to punch the tickets when you arrive.

Little Hands Story Corner™

Read *Hey! Get Off Our Train* by John Burningham and find out how a young boy who takes a trip on a toy train rescues endangered animals.

GARDEN CENTER

Do you love plants and flowers? Then you'll love visiting the local *garden nursery*, where you'll find many types of flowers, shrubs, and trees.

Why do you think it is called a *nursery?* Maybe because plants need a lot of love and care to grow big and strong, just like you do!

Fancy Flowered Hat

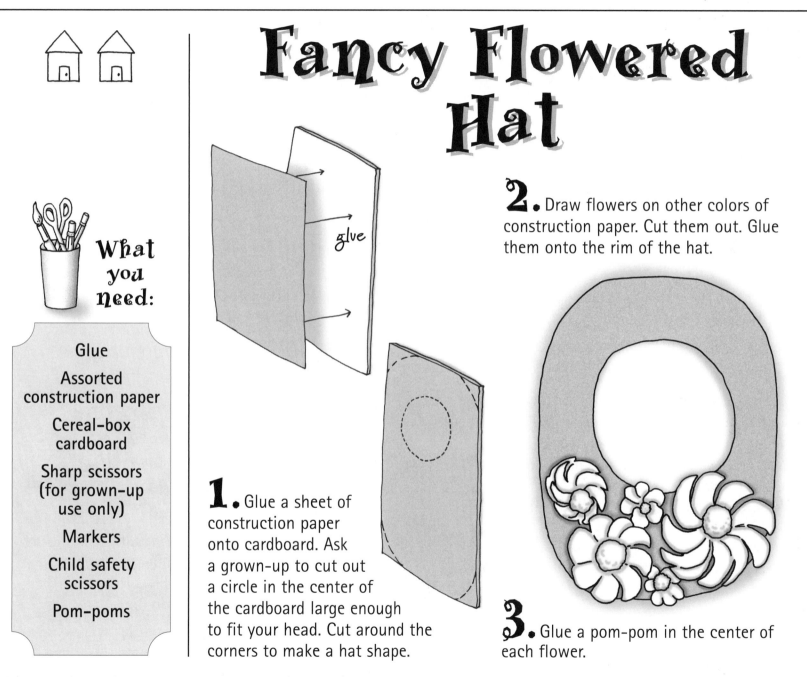

What you need:

Glue

Assorted construction paper

Cereal-box cardboard

Sharp scissors (for grown-up use only)

Markers

Child safety scissors

Pom-poms

glue

1. Glue a sheet of construction paper onto cardboard. Ask a grown-up to cut out a circle in the center of the cardboard large enough to fit your head. Cut around the corners to make a hat shape.

2. Draw flowers on other colors of construction paper. Cut them out. Glue them onto the rim of the hat.

3. Glue a pom-pom in the center of each flower.

When I grow up ...

I'll be a florist.

Florists run flower shops. They sell flowers and arrange bouquets and wreaths, too.

• **Make a flower change color.** Mix several drops of food coloring in a vase or jar of water. Put a light-colored cut flower, such as a carnation or daisy, in the water. Watch your flower change color!

• **Remove the stems from fresh flowers.** Place the flowers between several layers of old newspaper. Weigh them down with heavy books until they're flat and dry. Carefully place the flowers between two sheets of clear contact paper. Cut around the pressed flowers for bookmarks.

Be a good neighbor!

Offer to weed the gardens of elderly friends or neighbors. Before you begin, ask them to show you which plants to leave in the ground so you don't accidentally pull out the flowers!

Little Hands Story Corner™

Read *Alison's Zinnia* by Anita Lobel to see an alphabet of flowers. To find out how they grow, read *The Tiny Seed* by Eric Carle.

Plant a Flower Basket

Plant your seeds and water them to moisten. Set your cup in a sunny window. Keep the soil damp until the seeds sprout and then water as needed.

What you need:
Paper cup, potting soil, several flower seeds (marigolds, nasturtiums, and zinnias are colorful and easy to grow), strip of construction paper, stapler

Fill cup with soil.

Plant seeds about 1" (2.5 cm) deep.

Staple strip to cup.

Sun power!

Turn the cup so your little plant leans away from the window. When you check on it the next day, what do you notice? Your seedling is growing back toward the sunlight! You'll need to keep turning the cup so the plant's stem grows straight and strong.

Super Seedlings

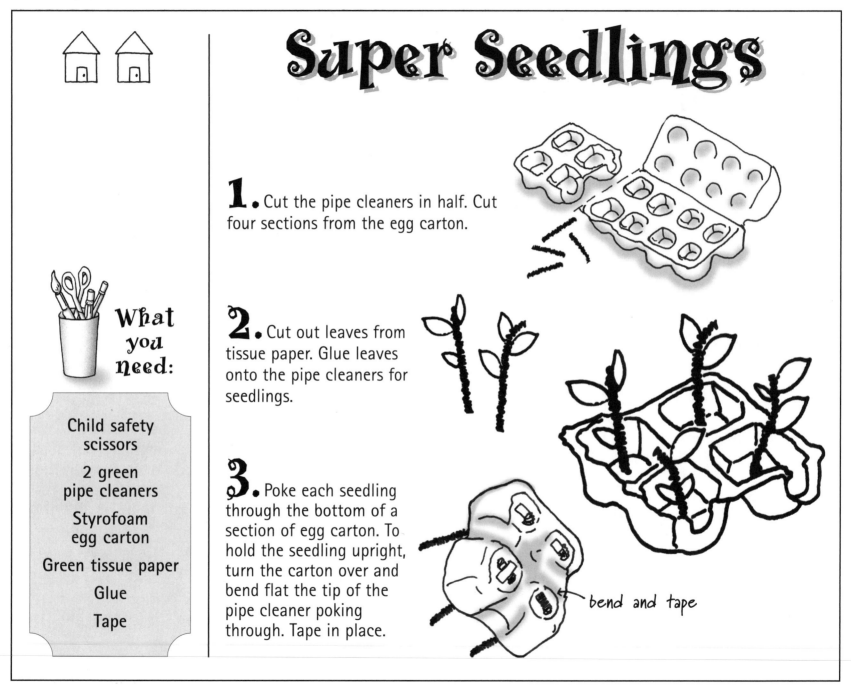

What you need:

Child safety scissors

2 green pipe cleaners

Styrofoam egg carton

Green tissue paper

Glue

Tape

1. Cut the pipe cleaners in half. Cut four sections from the egg carton.

2. Cut out leaves from tissue paper. Glue leaves onto the pipe cleaners for seedlings.

3. Poke each seedling through the bottom of a section of egg carton. To hold the seedling upright, turn the carton over and bend flat the tip of the pipe cleaner poking through. Tape in place.

bend and tape

When I grow up ...

I'll be a garden nursery worker. Nursery and greenhouse workers help to grow plants that are used to make our streets, sidewalks, parks, and outdoor areas pretty all year-round.

• **Put a wet sponge in a shallow dish.** Sprinkle easy-to-grow seeds (try marigold or zinnia seeds) in the holes of the sponge. Put the sponge on a plate and place it by a sunny window. Water every day so the sponge stays moist, but not wet. Watch the seeds start to grow; then, plant them in soil.

• **In the early spring, search for tree seedlings** before the lawn is mowed. Maple or elm tree seeds have bright green shoots close to the ground. Ask a grown-up if you can replant one where it can grow big and tall!

Be a good neighbor!

Keep off the grass! When you're in a hurry, don't cut across a neighbor's lawn. Stay on the sidewalk or keep to the path. Your neighbor will thank you!

Little Hands Story Corner™

Read *The Carrot Seed* by Ruth Krauss.

Seed Mosaic

Seeds come in all different shapes, sizes, and colors — how many different ways can you sort yours? Glue your seeds onto your paper to create different patterns or designs. Or, use the seeds to make a picture. It is easiest if you work on a small area at a time. When you make a picture using small pieces like this, the art you create is called a *mosaic*.

What you need: Variety of seeds, construction paper, glue

SENIOR CITIZENS' CENTER

Do you like playing with kids your own age? Guess what: So do older folks!

At the senior citizens' center, older people can make new friends their own age or learn a new skill or craft.

And one thing's for sure — the "seniors" always enjoy a visit from a friendly kid like you!

Magical Memory Album

What you need:

Glue

White paper

Assorted construction paper

Hole punch

Yarn or ring binders

Family photos

Markers

Ticket stubs, greeting cards, artwork

1. Glue white paper onto sheets of construction paper for the book's pages.

2. Punch three holes down the side of each sheet. Tie yarn through the holes to hold pages together.

3. Make copies of family photos. Glue the copies into the book. Use markers to write down what's happening in the photos, who the people are, or how old you were then.

4. Glue in birthday cards, your artwork, or ticket stubs from your favorite movies.

Be a good neighbor!

• **Save magazines and donate** them to a senior citizens' center.

• **Ask a grown-up to help you write a letter** to your grandparents. Tell them about your day and all the fun things you did. Illustrate your letter with pictures.

When I grow up ...

I'll be a physical therapist. Physical therapists help people recover from various illnesses and injuries by using massage, heat treatments, and exercises. They help people learn to move around again the way they did before they got hurt. Physical therapists at senior citizens' centers help elderly people exercise and keep their muscles and joints limber.

Olden Days

Talk to grandparents or other grown-ups about how times have changed since they were children. What kind of transportation did they use? What was the *same*, and what was *different?*

Little Hands Story Corner™

Read *Our Granny* by Margaret Wild to learn about grannies who come in different shapes and sizes.

Pom-Pom Picture Frame

1. Cut away the center of the paper plate without cutting through the side (you can ask a grown-up to help you get started).

2. Punch two holes in the top. Thread yarn through the holes to hang the frame. Glue pom-poms onto the frame. Let dry.

3. Trim the photo to fit the frame. Tape to hold in place on the back.

What you need:

Child safety scissors

Small white paper plate

Hole punch

Yarn

Glue

Pom-poms

Photo

Tape

Pasta & More Frames

Instead of pom-poms, glue sequins, dried pasta, paper curls, buttons, or stickers around the paper-plate frame.

When I grow up ...

I'll be a recreational therapist. Recreational therapists help people who have physical, emotional, and mental challenges with their disabilities. They teach leisure activities such as art and crafts and games, and they plan field trips so their clients can exercise and feel better.

Be a good neighbor!

• Volunteer, with a grown-up, at a senior citizens' center. Call out bingo numbers, play cards, and join in sing-a-longs with the residents. Bring along a cheery card you made and give it to one of the residents.

• "Adopt" a grandparent. Put together a "goody bag" for an elderly friend. Deliver it in person with a grown-up. Include pictures, a homemade treat, some special tea bags, a scented bar of soap, and a new magazine.

Little Hands Story Corner™

Read *Abuela* by Arthur Dorros.

Handprint Famiy Tree

What you need: Construction paper, markers, colorful construction-paper scraps, child safety scissors, glue, pencil or pen

Draw a tree trunk with branches.

Trace your hand onto colorful pieces of construction paper. Cut them out. Then, glue your paper hands to the tree branches.

Write the names of your family members on each hand.

TOWN HALL

Your local town hall is bustling with activity! That's where people register to vote and where they can learn about the history of a house or building.

People pay their taxes at the town hall, and that's where they meet to work on town business, organize events, and discuss important town issues. Some town halls have an office for the local sheriff, too.

Ask a grown-up to take you to your town hall. You might even be able to visit the mayor!

MAYOR'S OFFICE

Skyline Shapes

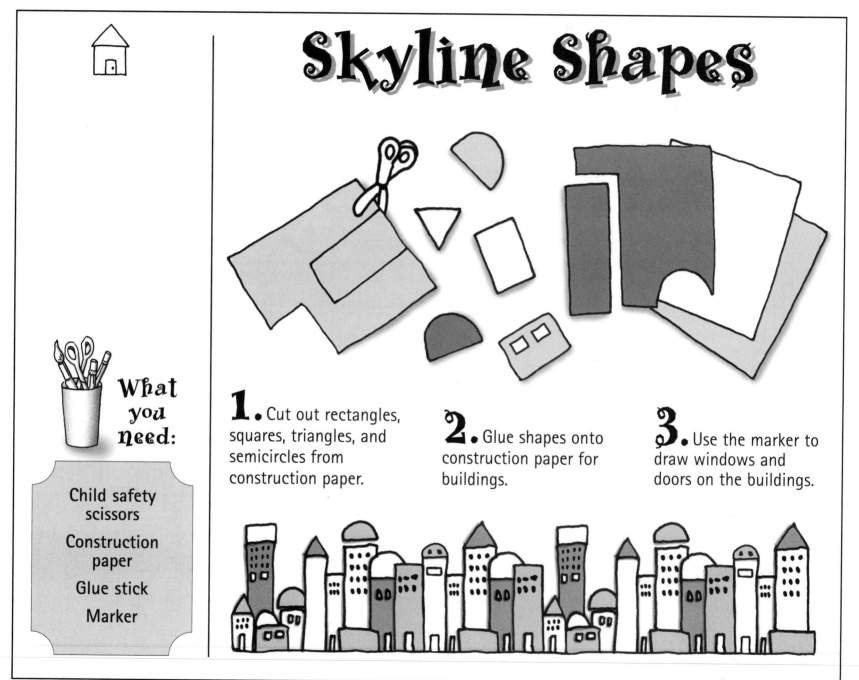

What you need:

Child safety scissors

Construction paper

Glue stick

Marker

1. Cut out rectangles, squares, triangles, and semicircles from construction paper.

2. Glue shapes onto construction paper for buildings.

3. Use the marker to draw windows and doors on the buildings.

Be a good neighbor!

Ask a grown-up to help you **write a letter to your community paper**, thanking someone in your town for all the hard work she does!

When I grow up ...

I'll be a town planner. Town planners help to make their communities as efficient and attractive as possible by planning where to put streets, parks, and neighborhoods.

• **Call your local library** to find out the web address of your town or city. There, you can learn about your community and the events going on in town!

• **Look for shapes** such as triangles, squares, and circles as you walk or ride around your city.

Little Hands Story Corner™

Read *The Little House* by Virginia Lee Burton to find out what a country house does when the city, with all its buildings and traffic, grows up around her.

"Order in the Court" Judge's Gavel

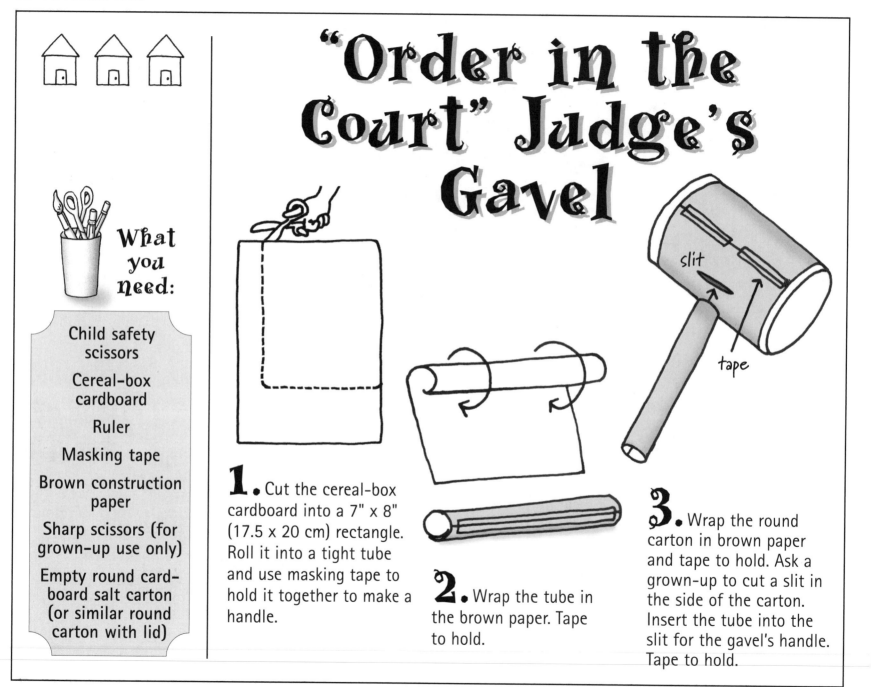

What you need:

- Child safety scissors
- Cereal-box cardboard
- Ruler
- Masking tape
- Brown construction paper
- Sharp scissors (for grown-up use only)
- Empty round cardboard salt carton (or similar round carton with lid)

1. Cut the cereal-box cardboard into a 7" x 8" (17.5 x 20 cm) rectangle. Roll it into a tight tube and use masking tape to hold it together to make a handle.

2. Wrap the tube in the brown paper. Tape to hold.

3. Wrap the round carton in brown paper and tape to hold. Ask a grown-up to cut a slit in the side of the carton. Insert the tube into the slit for the gavel's handle. Tape to hold.

slit

tape

Be a good neighbor!

Attend a town hall meeting with a grown-up to see how decisions are made in your community. The next time you and your friends have a misunderstanding, try to listen hard to the other person's point of view.

When I grow up ...

I'll be a judge. Judges interpret the law so that all people are treated fairly. When they're in their courtrooms, judges listen to *lawyers* who present both sides of a problem. Judges keep order in the court, handle disputes, and give advice to lawyers, juries, and people involved in lawsuits.

• **Hold a *mock* (pretend) court.** Agree to accept the decision of a judge; then, have each person tell her side of the story and wait for the *verdict* (decision).

Little Hands Story Corner™

Read *Why Are You Fighting, Davy?* by Brigitte Weninger for a story about *resolving conflicts* (solving arguments and fights).

GROCERY STORE

Lots of people grow, prepare, and package the food we eat. When they're done, they send it to the grocery store for people to buy.

In the produce section, you'll see fruits and vegetables; there's also the meat department, and the frozen foods section, where you'll find everything from frozen pizzas to orange juice in cans (and plenty of ice cream!). Which section do you like best?

FRUIT

Colorful Food Collage

What you need:

Child safety scissors

Old magazines

Glue stick

2 sheets of waxed paper

Old newspaper

Iron (for grown-up use only)

1. Cut out pictures and names of food from old magazines. Glue them onto one sheet of waxed paper. Lay the second sheet of waxed paper on top of your collage.

2. Place the waxed-paper sandwich between sheets of newspaper. Ask a grown-up to iron quickly back and forth over the newspaper. The heat from the iron will hold the waxed paper together. Trim the waxed paper.

When I grow up ...

I'll be a cashier. Cashiers scan or type the prices of the items being purchased, total the amount due, take money from customers, and give customers their receipts and the correct change.

• **Set up a pretend grocery store.** Save empty food boxes and stack them on a shelf. Then, go grocery shopping using play money.

• **Look through newspapers and flyers for coupons** for foods your family eats. Ask a grown-up to help you cut them out. Take them with you when you go to the grocery store and give them to the cashier when you check out. How much money did you save by using them?

Be a good neighbor!

Donate canned foods to your local food bank. Use cloth bags when you shop, and recycle your plastic and paper grocery bags, too.

Little Hands Story Corner™

Read *Eating the Alphabet: Fruits & Vegetables from A to Z* by Lois Ehlert for a delicious trip through the alphabet!

Vegetable Prints

What you need: Assorted vegetables (celery stalks, sliced mushrooms, green pepper rings, broccoli florettes), tempera paints, paper plates, white paper

1. Ask a grown-up to slice some vegetables or make a design on the flat surface of a potato half.

2. Pour a thin layer of tempera paint into a paper plate. Dip the flat sides of the vegetables into the paint.

3. Press onto paper for veggie prints.

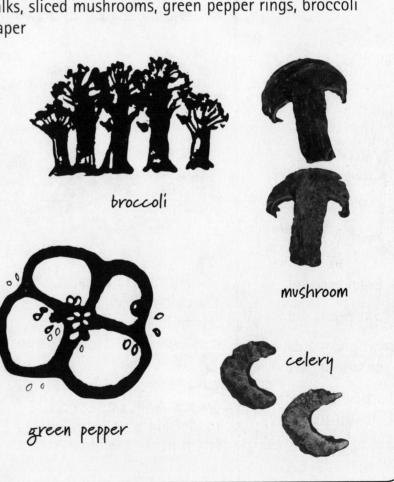

broccoli

mushroom

green pepper

celery

potato prints

Felt Fruit Bin

1. Use the marker to trace the shoe-box lid on a large piece of green felt. Ask a grown-up to help cut out the felt. Glue the felt to the inside of the box lid. Use the marker to draw three lines to separate the felt into different "bins."

What you need:

Black marker

Shoe-box lid

Green and assorted colors of felt

Sharp scissors (for grown-up use only)

Glue

draw lines

glue felt piece

2. Draw fruit shapes on the colored felt. Cut out the felt fruit.

3. Pretend you're the grocer. What's on special today? Place your favorite felt fruits in the bins!

When I grow up ... I'll be a grocery stock clerk. Stock clerks fill the shelves with food and other items and arrange the groceries in special displays to attract customers.

• **Play an alphabet game** when you're grocery shopping. Find a product that begins with the letter A. Then, move on to B and so on down the alphabet. What did you find for Q and Z?

Be a good neighbor!

Help unpack groceries at home. Put the fresh vegetables in a group near the refrigerator, the crackers and cereal near the correct cabinet, and all of the canned foods in one place.

Little Hands Story Corner™

Read *How Are You Peeling?* by Saxton Freymann to see some amazing photos of fruits and vegetables.

Yummy Snacks

Have a grown-up help you make these healthy treats using items you can buy at the grocery store!

Easy cranberry relish

What you need:
12 oz (300 g) cranberries, orange (peeled and seeded), 3/4 to 1 cup (150 to 200 g) sugar

Have a grown-up help you combine the cranberries, orange, and sugar in a blender or food processor. Serve the relish at Thanksgiving!

Banana goodies

Hungry little monkeys will gobble up these yummy banana snacks!

• Toss a banana in a blender with strawberries and yogurt for a quick and delicious fruit smoothie.

• Dip a banana in melted chocolate and then freeze it for a sweet treat.

• Fill a wooden skewer with sliced bananas, blueberries, and chunks of apples, pineapple, and kiwis for delicious fruit kabobs.

AIRPORT

Whoosh! Here comes a plane, landing on the run-way! And there's another one taking off!

And look at all the people coming and going! There are families heading off on vacation, people in suits with briefcases, travelers with backpacks, and airline workers checking the bags and tickets of people standing in line.

Where in the world would you like to fly? Perhaps to China, to see the panda bears in the great bamboo forests! Or maybe to Paris, France, to climb the Eiffel Tower! Or to London, to see the Queen!

Tickets →

Soaring Paper Airplane

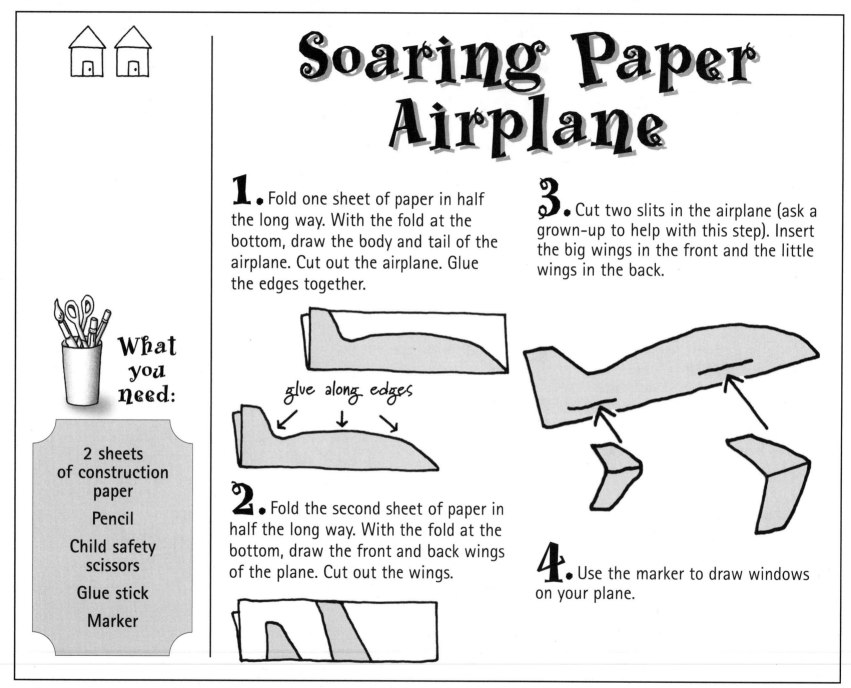

What you need:

2 sheets of construction paper

Pencil

Child safety scissors

Glue stick

Marker

1. Fold one sheet of paper in half the long way. With the fold at the bottom, draw the body and tail of the airplane. Cut out the airplane. Glue the edges together.

glue along edges

2. Fold the second sheet of paper in half the long way. With the fold at the bottom, draw the front and back wings of the plane. Cut out the wings.

3. Cut two slits in the airplane (ask a grown-up to help with this step). Insert the big wings in the front and the little wings in the back.

4. Use the marker to draw windows on your plane.

When I grow up ...

I'll be a pilot.

Commercial airline pilots fly large airplanes. They are in charge of their *crew* (the people who work on the plane), the plane, and the passengers they carry through the sky.

• **Have your friends** make their own paper airplanes. Hold a contest to see whose plane flies the farthest.

• **Design a** *logo* (symbol) for your own airline. Use markers to draw it on the side of your paper airplane.

• **Celebrate a special occasion** with a travel party. Send out invitations in the shape of an airplane. Ask each guest to wear an outfit they might wear on a faraway vacation!

Be a good neighbor!

Do you have a neighbor who goes away a lot? If so, ask a grown-up if you can volunteer to water her garden or feed his cat. What a nice neighbor you are!

Little Hands Story Corner™

Read *Ruth Law Thrills a Nation* by Don Brown to learn the story of an exciting historic flight by a daring woman!

High-in-the-Sky Control Tower

What you need:

- Child safety scissors
- 2 paper cups
- Paper-towel tube
- Recycled aluminum foil
- Tape
- Scrap of white paper
- Black marker

1. Cut away a large circle from the bottom of one cup. Wrap both cups and the paper-towel tube in the aluminum foil. Tape to hold.

2. Turn the cup with the hole upside down. Slide the tube through the hole. Tape the second cup to the top of the tube.

3. Use the marker to draw a door and windows on scrap paper. Cut them out and tape them onto the tower.

tape to hold

slide the tube in

Be a good neighbor!

Ask a friend or neighbor to play "If I could fly" with you. Let your friend go first and say: "If I could fly, I'd go to (name a place), with (name a person), to (say what you would do there). Then you take a turn.

When I grow up ...

I'll be an air traffic controller. Air traffic controllers watch the airplanes as they take off and land, and while they're in the air, too. They give directions to the pilots (page 95) who fly the planes so that everyone traveling in the air stays safe.

• **Air traffic controllers** need to know the strength and direction of the wind. Here's an easy way to find out which way the wind is blowing. Lick the tip of one finger and hold it above your head. When the finger is facing the wind, it will feel cool. Use a compass or ask a grown-up which direction the wind is coming from — north, south, east, or west.

Little Hands Story Corner™

Read *Up and Away: Taking a Flight* by Meredith Davis to learn about the different jobs people do at a busy airport and what happens on a passenger flight.

THEATER

Dancers, actors, musicians — performing artists of all kinds — entertain people at theaters.

On stage, live artists might dance a ballet or put on a play (you might even be in a performance there someday!).

When you're at a theater, do you like to sit way up close or far away?

Finger-Puppet Fun

What you need:

Glue stick

Large white envelope

Child safety scissors

Markers

Wiggly eyes (optional)

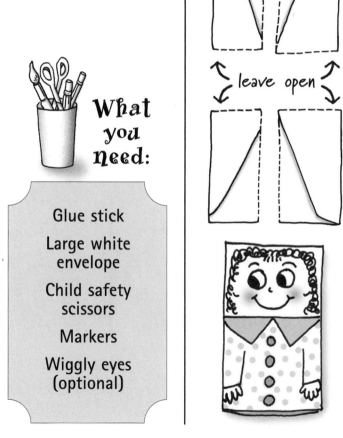

leave open

1. Glue down the flap of the envelope. Cut the envelope in half the long way. Cut each piece in half again horizontally. You should have four pieces.

2. Glue together the outside edges of each piece (leave the bottom open).

3. Use markers to draw the puppets. Draw or glue on the eyes.

Be a good neighbor!

Gather some friends to perform a **play or sing some songs** for kids and parents in your neighborhood. Or, check with a grown-up about performing the show at the local senior center. Make plans; then, create posters announcing the time and date. Rehearse your performance until it's near perfect. After the show, take a bow!

When I grow up ...

I'll be a puppeteer. Puppeteers make the puppets move, design costumes for them, and put on puppet shows.

• **Make puppets from wooden spoons.** Paint the wooden spoon different skin tones and allow to dry completely. Use markers to draw faces on the bowls of the spoons. Glue on yarn for puppet hair.

• **Make puppets of everyone in your family.** Perform a puppet show behind an old sheet hanging between two chairs.

• **Cut out the shape of an animal** from scrap cardboard and glue it onto a craft stick. Turn on a lamp and hold the stick so it casts a shadow on the wall. Then, perform a shadow-puppet show.

Little Hands Story Corner™

Read the classic story *Pinnochio* by C. Collodi and Ed Young.

"Handy" Finger-Puppet Theater

What you need:

Sharp scissors (for grown-up use only)

Empty cereal box

Glue

Construction paper

Markers

BACK

1. Cut away the lower half of the back of the box. Turn the box over and cut away the top half of the front.

FRONT

add curtains and a top

Theater

construction paper

2. Glue construction paper to the front of the box. Make curtains and a top from construction paper. Use markers to decorate.

Be a good neighbor!

Host a movie at home with your favorite video. Invite family and friends. Make tickets out of construction paper, serve popcorn, and show all of your guests to their seats, using a flashlight.

When I grow up ...

I'll be an usher.

Ushers work at movie theaters, plays, sporting events, and concerts. They collect admission tickets and help people to find their seats. You can usher your stuffed animals to a front-row seat and then perform a puppet show for them in your finger-puppet theater.

• Ask your teacher if you can be an usher on visiting day or Grandparents' Day at school.

Little Hands Story Corner™

Read *Shrinking Violet* by Cari Best to find out how Violet gets a special part in her class play.

ICE-CREAM SHOP

"**I** scream, you scream, we all scream for ice cream!" You've probably heard that one before. And who *wouldn't* get excited about all those tasty treats — cones, ice-cream cakes, frozen yogurt — and all those toppings!

Can you guess what flavors Americans like best?
#1 is vanilla
#2 is chocolate
#3 is butter pecan
#4 is strawberry
#5 is vanilla,
   chocolate,
   and strawberry
   combined

What's your
favorite?

Super Sundae

Pencil

Round lid

Assorted construction paper (white, pink, and brown — or any "flavor" you like!)

Child safety scissors

Glue

2 large white paper plates

Recycled aluminum foil

Stapler

Red pom-pom

1. Trace around the lid to make ice cream circles on the construction paper. Cut out the circles and glue them onto one paper plate.

2. Cut away one half of the second plate. Wrap it in foil. Staple it onto the first plate for a dish.

3. Glue a "cherry" pom-pom on top of the scoops of ice cream. Yum!

staple together

When I grow up ..

I'll be a soda jerk.

That's what your grandparents called a person who worked behind the counter serving ice-cream sodas, sundaes, and other ice-cream treats! It's a good job for teenagers who want to make spending money. These workers also do the dishes and keep the store clean.

• **Make up names of weird ice-cream flavors.** How about pickles and cream, chunky sauerkraut, and mint chip mustard? Ugh!

• **Make your own real ice-cream sundae.** Scoop balls of ice cream into a large serving bowl. Pour caramel or chocolate syrup over the top. Add bananas, strawberries, peaches, or blueberries. Then, add whipped cream and a cherry. Delicious!

Be a good neighbor!

Just about everyone enjoys an ice-cream treat! **Invite someone new to your street or apartment** to go out for ice cream with your family. Or, bring a neighbor an ice cream for a surprise on a hot day!

Little Hands Story Corner™

Read *Ice Cream Soup* by Frank Modell and find out how Marvin and Milton do making cake and ice cream for their own birthday party.

Yummy Ice-Cream Cone

What you need:

Brown construction paper

Child safety scissors

Black marker

Tape

Tissue paper

Glue

1. Fold the construction paper into a triangle. Cut off the long piece at the edge to make a square piece. Cut off one corner of the triangle.

fold

cut

cut

roll and tape

2. Use the marker to draw a waffle pattern. Roll the paper into the shape of a cone and tape to hold.

3. Scrunch the tissue paper into a ball. Glue the tissue paper inside the cone for a scoop of ice cream. What flavor did you make?

Be a good neighbor!

Ask a grown-up to explain the difference among **whole milk**, **1 percent milk**, and **skim milk**. Do you know which kind keeps you healthiest? If you said skim milk, you were right! Now tell a friend what you have learned.

When I grow up ...

I'll be a dairy farmer. Dairy farmers raise the cows that produce the milk to make ice cream. Farmers milk the cows twice a day, every day (even on holidays!). They set up and clean the milking equipment, and the milk is taken by refrigerated truck to the *bottling plant.* Can you guess what happens there?

• **How many products can you name** that are made from milk? How about cheese?

• **Cut out a rectangle** from brown construction paper. Cut around the corners for a chocolate-coated ice-cream bar. Glue the bar onto a Popsicle stick.

Little Hands Story Corner™

Read *Simply Delicious* by Margaret Mahy for an ice-cream adventure.

GAS STATION

Most cars and buses need gas to run. They won't get very far on empty!

Do you know how to tell if a car needs gas? Ask a grown-up to show you. If the tank is low, head off to the local gas station to fill it.

The workers at the gas station know all about how to take good care of cars and trucks — and even your bike, if the tires need air.

Cruise-Around Car

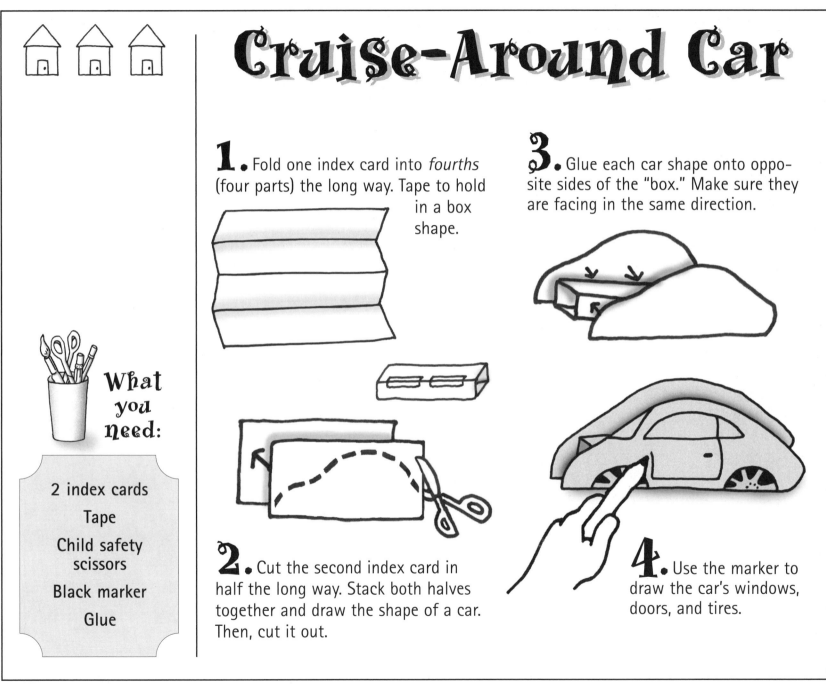

What you need:

2 index cards
Tape
Child safety scissors
Black marker
Glue

1. Fold one index card into *fourths* (four parts) the long way. Tape to hold in a box shape.

2. Cut the second index card in half the long way. Stack both halves together and draw the shape of a car. Then, cut it out.

3. Glue each car shape onto opposite sides of the "box." Make sure they are facing in the same direction.

4. Use the marker to draw the car's windows, doors, and tires.

Make a Tunnel

How about making a paper-bag tunnel for your cruise-around car (page 109)?

What you need: Child safety scissors, brown grocery bag, stapler

Cut the bottom off a brown grovery bag.

Cut the top in half the long way. Open both halves.

Lay one half on top of the other.

Fold up the sides and staple to hold.

Add some Pospicle trees (page 37) along the side.

When I grow up ...

I'll be a taxi driver. Taxi drivers help people get to where they need to go. They drive people to the airport, to the grocery store, to the bank, and then sometimes drive them home again in their big yellow taxis. They get to meet a lot of people in their work, including visitors from out of town and people from the community who don't have cars of their own.

• **Play a car color game.** The first one to count 10 cars of the same color wins!

• **Make a toy car wash.** Fill a spray bottle with soapy water. Wash your toy cars and trucks outside; then, dry them off with a towel.

Be a good neighbor!

Remind your friends (and grown-ups!) what the rules of the road are when crossing the street:
• Hold hands with a grown-up. Then, *stop, look, and listen* before you cross.

And when in a car, always buckle up for safety — and ask the grown-up to buckle up, too!

Little Hands Story Corner™

Read *Red, Yellow, Green — What Do Signs Mean?* by Joan Holub so you can read the signs on the road, just like a taxi driver!

Traffic Light

Drivers watch the traffic lights. The bottom one is green. Red is at the very top, and yellow's in-between!

What you need:
Quart (1 L) milk or juice carton, rinsed out and dried; black construction paper; tape; child safety scissors; red, yellow, and green construction paper; glue

1. Wrap the carton in black construction paper. Tape to hold.

2. Cut out red, yellow, and green construction-paper circles.

3. Glue circles onto the carton for a traffic light.

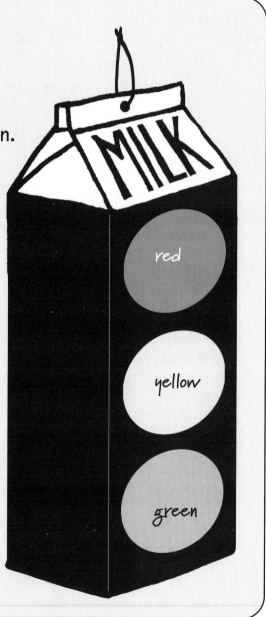

Twinkle, Twinkle, Little Stop Light

Sing this song to the tune of "Twinkle, Twinkle, Little Star"
as you play with your traffic light.

Twinkle, twinkle traffic light,
(form circle shape with hands)

Shining on the corner bright,

Stop shines red,
(hold hand out in "stop" motion)

Go is green,
(walk in place)

Slow-down yellow's in-between,
(walk slowly to a stop)

Twinkle, twinkle traffic light,
(form circle shape with hands)

Shining on the corner bright.

Ready-to-Go Gas Pump

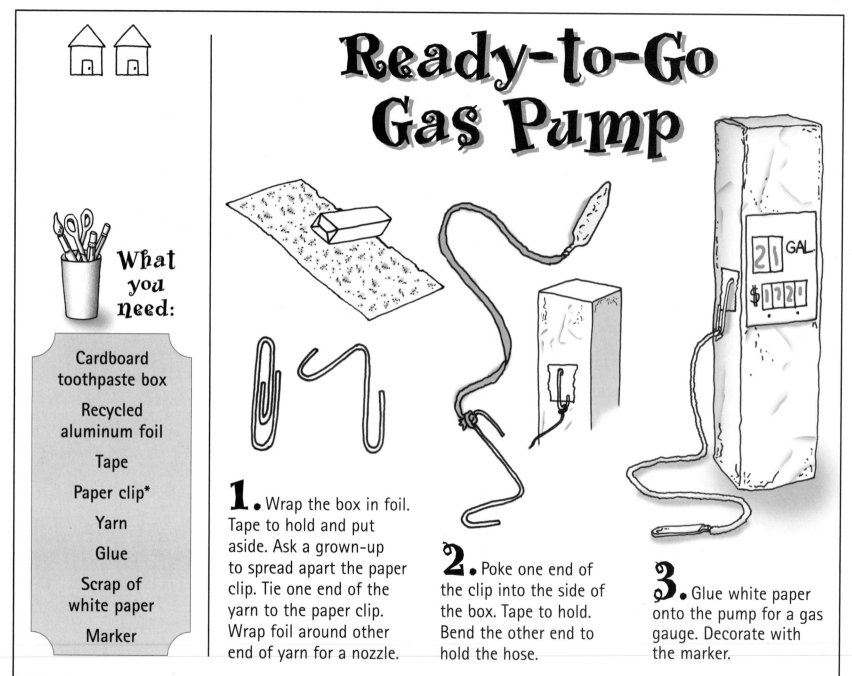

What you need:

Cardboard toothpaste box

Recycled aluminum foil

Tape

Paper clip*

Yarn

Glue

Scrap of white paper

Marker

1. Wrap the box in foil. Tape to hold and put aside. Ask a grown-up to spread apart the paper clip. Tie one end of the yarn to the paper clip. Wrap foil around other end of yarn for a nozzle.

2. Poke one end of the clip into the side of the box. Tape to hold. Bend the other end to hold the hose.

3. Glue white paper onto the pump for a gas gauge. Decorate with the marker.

*Caution: Paper clips pose a choking and poking danger to young children. Grown-ups should control the supply and insert them into the project.

Be a good neighbor!

Ask a grown-up to help you check the air in your friends' bicycle tires. If any are low, ask a grown-up to help you take them to a gas station to fill the tires up at the air pump.

When I grow up ...

I'll be an auto mechanic. Auto mechanics fix cars when they break down or are in an accident. They give cars regular tune-ups to fix engine parts that aren't working properly.

• Ask a grown-up to show you the inside of a car under the hood.

Little Hands Story Corner™

Read *Lucky's 24-Hour Garage* by Daniel Kirk to learn about Angelo, a gas station attendant.

Stop Sign

You can stay safe by paying attention to this road sign, whether you're in a car or on your bike!

What you need:
Child safety scissors, red and white construction paper, glue, cardboard paper-towel tube, tape

Cut out a circle from red construction paper.

Cut the letters S, T, O, and P from white paper. Glue the letters onto the red circle.

Cut a slit in the top of a paper-towel tube. Tape the circle into the slit for a stop sign.

Cardboard Carton Obstacle Course

What you need:
Large cardboard boxes, tempera paint, large paintbrush, heavy paper plate, old newspaper

1. Cover the floor with old newspaper. Pour a small amount of paint into the paper plate. Paint the cartons. Let dry.

2. Place boxes in an obstacle course formation; then ride your tricycles around them.

3. Practice your driving in a homemade obstacle course!

Don't forget the safe-biking rule: Always wear a helmet!

RESTAURANT

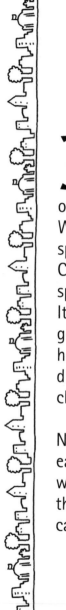

Do you like to eat out at a restaurant? What's your favorite — spring rolls from a Chinese restaurant, spaghetti from an Italian restaurant, or a good old-fashioned hamburger at the local diner or fast-food chain?

No matter where you eat, a look at the menu will tell you about all the delicious foods you can enjoy!

Dish-It-Up Chef's Hat

What you need:

Child safety scissors

White construction paper

Tape

White paper gift bag

Sharp scissors (for grown-up use only)

Stapler

1. Cut the construction paper in half the long way. Tape the short ends together on one side. Ask a grown-up to adjust the length to fit around your head. Tape the ends together.

2. Ask a grown-up to help you cut the handles off the bag. Hold the paper bag upside down. Insert the paper bag inside the paper band.

3. Staple the bag along the bottom edge of the paper collar.

staple on dotted line

High Hat

Can you guess why a chef's hat is so tall? It helps keep a cook's head cool while he works around a hot stove and oven. Can you think of other hat designs that help to keep your head safe or cool?

When I grow up ...

I'll be a chef. Chefs wake up bright and early and go to the market to buy fresh food. Back in the kitchen, they chop and slice ingredients, preparing them to make the yummy meals on the menu.

• **Make a fruit salad.** You can peel the bananas and wash the grapes while a grown-up cuts the fruit. Toss it together, then serve it to your friends and family as if they were in a restaurant.

Be a good neighbor!

Volunteer at school to collect food for the community food shelf. Ask your classmates to bring in one can of food each week. Then, ask a grown-up to help you deliver the food. Congratulations! You are a helpful member of your community.

Little Hands Story Corner™

Read *Felix's Cookbook* by Annette Langen for some little kid–friendly tasty treats to make in your own pretend restaurant.

Make Some Butter

Serve tea, toast, jam, and some homemade butter to a neighbor or special friend.

What you need:
½ cup (125 ml) heavy cream, 1 tablespoon (15 ml) sour cream, jar with lid, spoon, saucer, salt (optional)

1. Ask a grown-up to pour the cream and sour cream into the jar. Cover the jar tightly and shake it hard. Keep shaking or take turns shaking with a few friends. Watch as you shake up the jar.

2. After a long while, you'll see soft butter at the bottom of the jar. Pour off the leftover liquid and place the butter in a saucer. Press the butter firmly with the rounded back of a spoon to drain the rest of the liquid.

3. Guess what? You've made your own delicious butter! Invite a special some-one to share it with you.

Pizza, Pizza Pie!

What you need:

Red, brown, and black crayons or markers

Large white paper plate

Child safety scissors

White tissue paper

Glue

Scraps of brown, white, green, and black construction paper

1. Color the center of the paper plate red. Color the rim of the plate brown. Draw slices with the black marker.

2. Cut thin strips of tissue paper. Glue tissue strips onto the plate for "cheese."

3. Top it off. Cut out small circles from brown paper. Glue the circles onto the plate for "pepperoni." Cut out different toppings and glue them onto your pizza. How about mushrooms, peppers, or olives?

Be a good neighbor!

Serve breakfast in bed to someone special. Add a special touch by putting a fresh flower in a vase and placing it on the tray.

When I grow up ...

I'll be a waitperson. Waitpeople work in places where people can sit down to eat. They set the tables with silverware, plates, and glasses. They show customers to their tables, give them menus, and write down their orders. When the food is ready, they serve it. After the meal they clear away the dirty plates and present the bill.

• **Plan your family dinner** as if you were in a restaurant. Write the menu on a sheet of paper. Set the table and take the orders. Don't forget to clear off the table when everyone's done!

Little Hands Story Corner™

Read *Pete's a Pizza* by William Steig to find out how a boy's father turns him into a pizza.

Craft Index by Skill Level

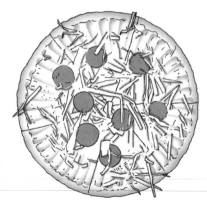

Activity Index

Williamson's *Kids Can!* Books

To order, see page 128.

The following Williamson *Kids Can!* books for ages 6 to 13 are each 144 to 176 pages, fully illustrated, trade paper, 11 x 8¹/₂, $12.95 US/$19.95 CAN.

AWESOME OCEAN SCIENCE!
Investigating the Secrets of the Underwater World
by Cindy A. Littlefield

Parents' Choice Recommended
KIDS' ART WORKS!
Creating with Color, Design, Texture & More
by Sandi Henry

Parents' Choice Gold Award
Benjamin Franklin Best Juvenile Nonfiction Award
KIDS MAKE MUSIC!
Clapping and Tapping from Bach to Rock
by Avery Hart & Paul Mantell

Oppenheim Toy Portfolio Best Book Award
Parents' Choice Approved
SUMMER FUN!
60 Activities for a Kid-Perfect Summer
by Susan Williamson

KIDS COOK!
Fabulous Food for the Whole Family
by Sarah Williamson & Zachary Williamson

HANDS AROUND THE WORLD
365 Creative Ways to Build Cultural
Awareness & Global Respect
by Susan Milord

REAL-WORLD MATH FOR HANDS-ON FUN!
by Cindy A. Littlefield

Parents Magazine Parents' Pick Award
Real Life Award
KIDS LEARN AMERICA!
Bringing Geography to Life with People,
Places & History
by Patricia Gordon & Reed C. Snow

Parents' Choice Recommended
THE KIDS' BOOK OF WEATHER FORECASTING
Build a Weather Station, "Read" the Sky
& Make Predictions!
with meteorologist Mark Breen & Kathleen Friestad

American Bookseller Pick of the Lists
Dr. Toy Best Vacation Product
KIDS' CRAZY ART CONCOCTIONS
50 Mysterious Mixtures for Art & Craft Fun
by Jill Frankel Hauser

American Institute of Physics Science Writing Award
Parents' Choice Honor Award
GIZMOS & GADGETS
Creating Science Contraptions that Work
(& Knowing Why)
by Jill Frankel Hauser

Parents' Choice Gold Award
Oppenheim Toy Portfolio Best Book Award
THE KIDS' MULTICULTURAL ART BOOK
Art & Craft Experiences from Around the World
by Alexandra M. Terzian

**The Kids' Guide to Making
SCRAPBOOKS & PHOTO ALBUMS!**
How to Collect, Design, Assemble, Decorate
by Laura Check

GREAT GAMES!
Old & New, Indoor/Outdoor, Board, Card, Ball & Word
by Sam Taggar

THE KIDS' MULTICULTURAL COOKBOOK
Food & Fun Around the World
by Deanna F. Cook

HAND-PRINT ANIMAL ART
by Carolyn Carreiro

THE KIDS' WILDLIFE BOOK
Exploring Animal Worlds through
Indoor/Outdoor Crafts & Experiences
by Warner Shedd

Prices may be slightly higher when purchased in Canada.

The following **Quick Starts for Kids!**™ books for children, ages 8 and older, are each 64 pages, fully illustrated, trade paper, 8 x 10, $7.95 US/$10.95 CAN.

DRAWING HORSES
(that look *real!*)
by Don Mayne

MAKE YOUR OWN CHRISTMAS ORNAMENTS
by Ginger Johnson

REALLY COOL FELT CRAFTS
by Peg Blanchette & Terri Thibault

Parents' Choice Approved
BAKE THE BEST-EVER COOKIES!
by Sarah A. Williamson

BE A CLOWN!
Techniques from a Real Clown
by Ron Burgess

Oppenheim Toy Portfolio Best Book Award
DRAW YOUR OWN CARTOONS!
by Don Mayne

40 KNOTS TO KNOW
Hitches, Loops, Bends & Bindings
by Emily Stetson

GARDEN FUN!
Indoors & Out; In Pots and Small Spots
by Vicky Congdon

KIDS' EASY KNITTING PROJECTS
by Peg Blanchette

KIDS' EASY QUILTING PROJECTS
by Terri Thibault

Dr. Toy 100 Best Children's Products
Dr. Toy 10 Best Socially Responsible Products
MAKE YOUR OWN BIRDHOUSES & FEEDERS
by Robyn Haus

MAKE YOUR OWN FUN PICTURE FRAMES!
by Matt Phillips

MAKE YOUR OWN HAIRWEAR!
Beaded Barrettes, Clips, Dangles & Headbands
by Diane Baker

American Bookseller Pick of the Lists
MAKE YOUR OWN TEDDY BEARS & BEAR CLOTHES
by Sue Mahren

YO-YO!
Tips & Tricks from a Real Pro
by Ron Burgesss

Visit Our Website!
To see what's new at Williamsonand learn more about specific books, visit our website at:
<www.williamsonbooks.com>

To Order Books:
Toll-free phone orders with credit cards: **1-800-234-8791**
We accept Visa and MasterCard
(please include the number and expiration date).

Or, send a check with your order to:
Williamson Publishing Company
P.O. Box 185 • Charlotte, Vermont 05445

Catalog request: mail, phone, or e-mail <**info@williamsonbooks.com**>.

Please add $4.00 for postage for one book plus $1.00 for each additional book. Satisfaction is guaranteed or full refund without questions or quibbles.